P9-AOH-067

The
Vegan Family Cookbook

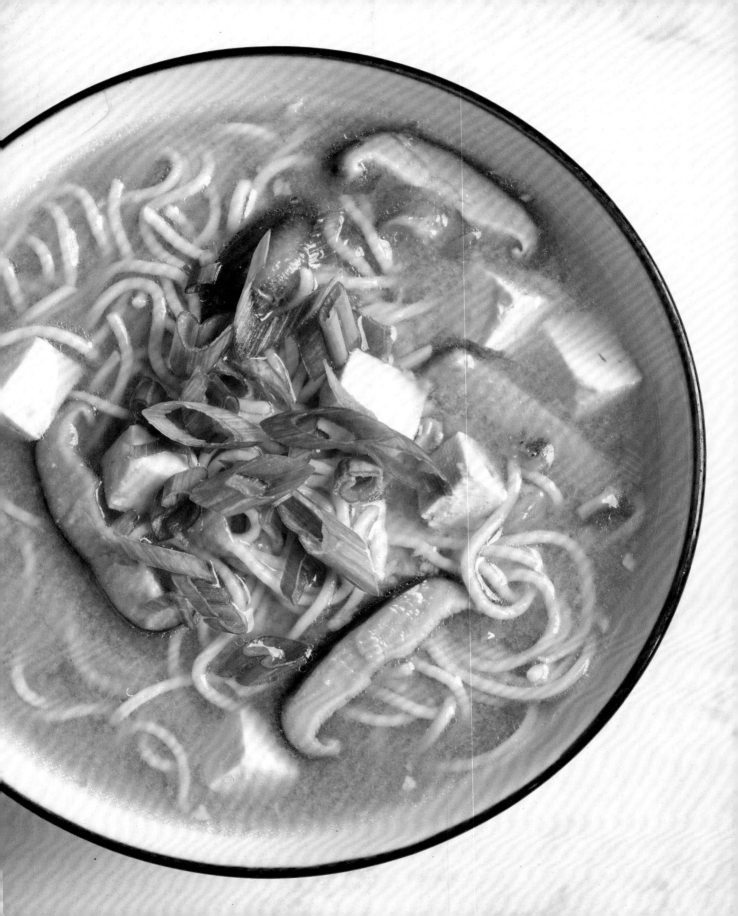

The
Vegan
Family
Cookbook

*Simple, Balanced Cooking
for Real Life*

Anna Pippus

appetite
by RANDOM HOUSE

Copyright © 2021 Anna Pippus

All rights reserved. The use of any part of this publication, reproduced, transmitted
in any form or by any means, electronic, mechanical, photocopying, recording,
or otherwise, or stored in a retrieval system, without the prior written consent of the
publisher—or, in case of photocopying or other reprographic copying, license from
the Canadian Copyright Licensing Agency—is an infringement of the copyright law.

Appetite by Random House® and colophon are registered trademarks
of Penguin Random House LLC.

Library and Archives Canada Cataloguing in Publication is available upon request.
ISBN: 9780147531308
eBook ISBN: 9780147531315

Cover and interior design: Leah Springate
Cover and interior photography: Anna Pippus
Photograph on page 4 by Shannon Nickerson

Printed in China

Published in Canada by Appetite by Random House®,
a division of Penguin Random House Canada Limited.

www.penguinrandomhouse.ca

10 9 8 7 6 5 4 3 2 1

appetite
by RANDOM HOUSE | Penguin
Random House
Canada

To Arden, Harlan, and Alister—
Thank you for giving me a family to feed

Contents

Introduction

Whether you're vegan, vegan-ish, trying to eat more plant foods like vegetables and legumes, or simply interested in eating well with minimal fuss—welcome! This book is for you.

I've been vegetarian for most of my life, for reasons that have evolved as I have. As a child, I had a strong connection to animals, from hamsters to horses. I loved them, but more than that, I related to them as emotional beings. I could see that, just like us humans, animals experience contentment, loneliness, excitement, boredom, fear, and relational connection. When I learned that vegetarians existed, I decided to become one; I didn't want to eat these miraculous creatures who were my friends.

As a teenager, I had a limited cooking repertoire. Fortunately, I still managed to absorb an appreciation of both cooking and eating from my parents, who are skilled cooks. Although my parents weren't vegetarian, they wholeheartedly supported me in expressing my values in this way. My dad would experiment with dishes like eggplant moussaka with béchamel sauce, and mushroom risotto with truffle oil. My mum often had a pot of legume-based soup simmering on the stove: French-inspired lentil, or black bean and spinach. I learned that cooking at home can be fun and creative, and even an expression of love.

When I moved out on my own, I started to cook more seriously for myself. As a vegetarian, I turned to Indian cuisine, with its endless inspiration for flavouring vegetables, grains, and legumes. I fried mustard seeds and turmeric with cauliflower, transformed spinach into fragrant sauce, braised cabbage with cumin seeds until it nearly melted, and cooked countless pots of lentils, starting with that all-important flavour foundation of sautéed onion, garlic, and spices. I was in awe that such bold, satisfying flavours could be created so simply, with so few ingredients. A sense of curiosity and experimentation in the kitchen took hold and has never left me.

I worked in restaurants to help put myself through school—first an undergraduate degree in psychology, then a juris doctorate in law. Although at the time, the restaurant jobs felt incidental to my "real" life, in retrospect I can see how being immersed in food culture further shaped how I cook and eat, and planted the seeds for what would become a career. I tasted delectable food prepared by veteran chefs, saw how ingredients could be transformed into beautiful plates of food, and learned how to analyze and talk about what makes a meal delicious.

As a law student, I learned more about farming and food systems. I was devastated to learn how destructive modern agriculture could be for workers, the environment, our health, and animals. I discovered that dairy and egg farming, even under best-case scenarios, involved practices that didn't sit well with my animal-loving self: animals are selectively bred, separated from their families, and killed in industrial slaughterhouses when their production declines. Males, of no use for dairy and eggs, are killed even sooner than are the females. I decided to boycott these industries, too, and became vegan. If there's one thing I love more than food, it's animals, and so the transition felt easy for me.

I was upset that I had unwittingly been contributing to this system, and I felt that the truth had been obscured from me—by cultural songs, books, and imagery that depict farming idealistically and falsely; by a sophisticated industrial agriculture industry with big marketing and lobbying budgets; and by a government that I had wrongly assumed was regulating sensitive industries. I felt driven to help educate people about modern food systems and to provide solutions. I started a (now-defunct) cooking blog, helped run an animal-law club, wrote most of my upper-year law school papers on animal rights topics, joined the board of a vegetarian organization, and held vegan-cooking classes and potlucks in the tiny home I shared with my husband, Arden. When it came time to start my legal career, there was never really any question that I would work in the area of farmed-animal protection.

Working as a farmed-animal lawyer strengthened my commitment to plant-based eating as a way to have a positive impact in our world. Time and again I saw how complicated and entrenched the problems of animal farming were, and how elegantly simple one solution could be: Get more people eating more plants. Through my work, I connected with many people who wanted to eat fewer animal foods but were genuinely stumped as to what to eat or even where to start. Most of us understand that eating more plants is a good thing, for our health, for the environment, for workers, and for animals. We don't need the why—we need the *how*.

In our information culture, we're inundated with websites and cookbooks with millions of plant-based recipes, but in spite of all this information—or perhaps because of it—it's difficult to figure out how to apply it to our own lives. I once had a shelf full of cookbooks and a browser full of bookmarked recipes, yet despite being a competent home cook, too many days I blanked at dinnertime. I'd make ravioli from scratch one day and order Thai food the next, burnt-out from my marathon cooking project. Every evening, after a long day at school or work, the same overwhelming question: What should we have for dinner?

Then, as a new mother on a tight budget and with my husband, Arden, working long hours out of the house, I was happily forced to take control in the kitchen. By challenging myself to cook all our meals every day, I honed some serious kitchen management skills. And it was an epiphany for me to realize that they *are* skills. Cooking dinner is easy, all things considered. What's difficult is deciding what to cook (arguably the hardest part right there), ensuring the ingredients are on-hand and fresh when you need them, and finding ways to use or repurpose ingredients and leftovers to avoid waste.

I no longer blank at dinnertime. I've found an approach to cooking that works for our family, and have a repertoire of simple, pantry-friendly meals. I love tasty food, I enjoy being in the kitchen, and I crave a varied diet. At the same time, I gravitate toward efficiency. Spending hours making a fiddly, gourmet feast is *not* my idea of a good time. I naturally seek out ways to minimize the time and effort put into cooking while not sacrificing flavour and satiety.

> In 2016, I started *Easy Animal-Free* as an Instagram account to share this approach to cooking that was working so well for me.

In 2016, I started *Easy Animal-Free* as an Instagram account to share this approach to cooking that was working so well for me. I thought it would be useful to provide an example of how one family of four managed the daily and weekly rhythms of animal-free eating. I wanted to show *how* we ate well with minimal effort—meals that are nutritionally balanced, family-friendly, tasty, satisfying, and practical for everyday people with full lives. I also hoped to inspire people to cook regularly, and to do so with confidence and resourcefulness—with or without recipes. I committed to sharing only food that my family really eats: real-world tested and family-approved.

Eating animal-free isn't a deprivation. On the contrary, putting vegetables, legumes, grains, spices, and herbs first opens us up to a world of fresh and exciting flavours. As award-winning authors Karen Page and Andrew Dornenburg put it in *The Vegetarian Flavor Bible*, one good reason for cooking plant-based is "maximizing flavor—which is too often masked by meat-based stocks or butter and cream."

The Easy Animal-Free project has grown into this very book. After years of sharing kitchen tips, hacks, and recipes in a piecemeal way, and after receiving dozens of polite messages from people sick of screen-shotting my content and asking me to please put it into a book already, the time felt right to organize it all into something more digestible. This book is a collection of my family's favourite foods and an articulation of how I approach making them. I hope it helps make it easier for you to eat more delicious plants. More than that, I hope it helps you find your own sense of joy and ease in the kitchen. Let me show you what I've learned.

Spanning decades of questionable fashion choices, my love of animals is unchanging.

How to Use This Book

This book is an invitation to peek into my family's kitchen, to share with you how we really make it work day to day and week to week. With that in mind, I organized the book according to how we cook and eat in real life. We enjoy breakfast-y foods in the morning, and often brunch on the weekends. If lunch isn't leftovers, it needs to be quick, portable, or sometimes both. I do the bulk of my cooking during the week, when I cook dinners by theme. We have pasta on Mondays, bowls on Tuesdays, one-pot meals on Wednesdays, and stir-fries or other pan-Asian–inspired meals on Thursdays. (I talk more about cooking by theme on page 10.) I don't plan anything for the weekends. We have a few go-to snacks for our active and hungry crew, and occasionally we like something sweet. On the following pages, I've also included plenty of general cooking guides, like how to cook dried beans (page 133), and templates, like how to make a bowl (page 127). You don't have to cook like me to make use of this book, of course. The recipes can be adapted to your own lifestyle, even if you—*gasp*—eat pasta on a Thursday.

A few general recipe notes

Salt and pepper. Often, I haven't specified a quantity for these. Some ingredients (canned tomatoes, canned beans, prepared stock) may already contain salt, and in varying amounts; people also have different sodium needs. As for pepper, spice tolerance levels are so variable. When I cook, I add a just little pepper, for the sake of my spice-averse littlest one, then put the pepper grinder on the table for the rest of us. For recipes where I do specify a salt quantity, you should know that I use fine-grain salt. If you're using a coarse grain, you may need more (although salt, and anything else really, is always to taste).

Spicy ingredients. I've gone easy on the spicy elements in these recipes because I cook for kids. I personally love spicy foods and add heat—via crushed red chilies, hot sauce, and spicy pickles—at the table. Please add chilies right into your cooking if you prefer.

Onions. For cooking, any mature onions will do—I usually use white or yellow, whichever feels firmest and looks freshest at the market when I'm shopping. Red onions may turn a swampy blue colour if you cook them in an alkaline dish, which is harmless but a little unappetizing. For raw onions, I prefer white or red.

Soy sauce. This ingredient is supposed to be fermented, which is key for its incredible complex and savoury flavour. Some of what is labelled as soy sauce is a non-fermented imitation, using additives for flavour. Look for "naturally brewed" or similar on the label, and check that the ingredients don't contain caramel colour or other additives. Soy sauce can be swapped for tamari.

Peanut butter. What I use is made from one ingredient: peanuts. Peanut butter with icing sugar, palm oil, or anything else added will not perform the same in my recipes.

Beans. Most of the time, I cook beans from dried. You can absolutely use canned beans instead. When recipes call for bean cooking liquid, use canned beans that contain no preservatives such as disodium EDTA or calcium chloride, which negatively impact flavour. Alternatively, rinse the canned beans and use water or stock in place of the bean cooking liquid. I provide measurements in both cups and millilitres for beans; here are a couple of conversions you'll come across:

- 14 oz (398 mL) cans contain about 1½ cups (375 mL) of beans
- 19 oz (540 mL) cans contain about 2 cups (500 mL) of beans

Oil. First and foremost, you should use what you have and what you like. Nobody needs a cupboard full of different oils for cooking. Take care to keep oil below its smoke point, though. I use extra virgin olive oil as my all-purpose oil—it has a smoke point of up to 410°F (210°C), depending on the particular oil—because it's a nutritious choice, being anti-inflammatory and a source of vitamins E and K. It isn't a neutral oil, though I personally like its mildly fruity, peppery, or grassy flavour in savoury cooking. I use refined avocado oil for very-high-heat cooking because its smoke point is around 520°F (270°C). Feel free to sub out oils for whatever suits you best.

What's an Oil Smoke Point?

The smoke point is the temperature at which an oil begins to smoke. It's impossible to pin down the exact smoke point of any type of oil, because the smoke point depends on how the oil is produced. It's not the oil itself that smokes but compounds within the oil—so very-unrefined oil will generally smoke at lower temperatures. When oil smokes, it's because compounds in it are burning, which results in a bitter taste and degrades the nutritional benefits of the oil. This, by the way, is why Indians use ghee—it's butter with some milk solids removed so the fat can tolerate a relatively high cooking heat. This is also why refined oils, while maybe not the optimally healthful choice for consuming raw, may be a better choice for high-heat cooking, like stir-frying or broiling. Most oils have a smoke point in the range of 300°F to 400°F (150°C to 200°C),[1] which also happens to be the temperature range in which we cook most food on the stove and in the oven.

If the manufacturer hasn't provided its oil's smoke point, the only sure way to know it is to cook with it, and to use your eyes and nose to determine if it's smoking. If your oil starts to smoke, immediately dial down the heat and either cook at a lower temperature or wipe out the pan and start again with a different oil.

Getting Started

In my family, I joke that I'm the kitchen manager. (Except I am *not joking*, because it is a legit job and I need business cards.) The challenging part of making dinner regularly is not so much the making of the dinner—it's deciding what to make, ensuring the ingredients are on-hand and fresh, and using or repurposing leftovers and odds and ends before they go to waste. It takes effort and skill to balance these essential tasks, especially in a high-volume kitchen.

I don't do most of the cooking and kitchen management in our home because I'm a woman; I do it because I love to do it. My husband, Arden, is my equal partner in all things family and home, and we divide tasks according to what we like and are good at. We prefer to have our domains that we're responsible for, which saves us from constantly consulting with each other about tedious little things and leaves us more time and mental bandwidth for things that matter more to us.

You will likely divide things up differently in your home, according to your own unique factors: How many household members are cooking? How many household members *enjoy* cooking? Does it work better for you to split tasks for the sake of variety, or have each person responsible for certain tasks to keep things streamlined? Are there kids at home, and if so, are they old enough to contribute—or, conversely, are they so young that they slow you down? What are the work hours of household members, and do they work at home or commute?

However you approach kitchen management, if there are other people old enough to contribute, I suggest you have a conversation with them about how you will divide kitchen tasks—and be prepared to switch things up as your circumstances evolve. Much of the labour of managing the kitchen is invisible, and it won't necessarily be apparent to your cohabitants that, say, your Sunday nights are plagued with thoughts of what to pack for lunches this week.

What's for dinner?

Early in my kitchen management career (ahem), I tried to make myself into a meal planner. On Saturday mornings, I diligently sat down with a stack of cookbooks and a list of our favourite recipes and made a list of what we'd cook for the week. Then I made a grocery list, which we'd shop for over the weekend.

This lasted for about 5 minutes. I found I couldn't stick with it—I dreaded the meal-planning marathon, weekend travel would totally throw us off for the week, and I didn't always feel like making or eating what was planned, for any number of reasons that are common in the homes of young families. (Lack of sleep! Unanticipated work complications! Fussy babies! Impromptu visitors or social plans!) I found it mentally draining to come up with a varied yet cohesive menu each week that wouldn't be too homogeneous nor too disparate, thus resulting in an assortment of leftover parts that couldn't work together. I needed something more realistic, flexible, and forgiving.

Then I discovered—or rather, remembered—cooking by theme. Your grandparents may have done it, or even your parents. Cooking by theme simply means assigning a general meal theme to a day of the week. If you've ever consistently had a roast on Sunday, tacos on Tuesday, or pizza on Friday, you've enjoyed the glory of themed meals. Done well, cooking by theme gives you a little direction without feeling onerous, and with loose enough themes, it doesn't get repetitive.

Here's how I do it:

Mondays are pasta. Pasta is generally super easy and fast to make, requiring few parts, which I appreciate on that weekend shoulder day. We really s-l-o-w it down on weekends and often eat at strange times (brunch and linner, anyone?). So on Mondays, boiling some noodles and putting a sauce on them feels about the right speed to ease us back into the faster pace of the week. Some of our fave easy pastas are my Basic Cashew Cream Pasta (page 108), Mushroom, Pinto Bean, and Tomato Pasta (page 116), and Lighter Kale Pesto Pasta (page 120).

Tuesdays are bowls. Bowls require a few more pots and pans and a little more consideration than other meals might. I can handle this on Tuesdays when I'm fully into weekday mode, and energy and creativity are most likely to be running high. I also like doing bowls on Tuesday because I can make extra components, which can be repurposed throughout the rest of the week for quick at-home and packed lunches. Our fave bowls are Mexican or Mediterranean inspired.

Wednesdays are one-pot meals. For one thing, I like the alliteration of "one-pot Wednesdays," because I'm a certified nerd. Mostly, they're cozy dinners that stock our fridge with leftovers for the rest of the week. Some people prefer to make a big pot of something on Sundays, when they have more time; if this is you, by Wednesday you'll feel ready to eat it again. A few go-to one-pot meals are Corn Soup with Sneaky Red Lentils (page 172), Black Bean and Tomato Soup with Toasted Fennel Seed (page 179), and The Easiest Curried Red Lentils (page 181), all of which can be made in 30 minutes or less.

Thursdays we have stir-fries or other pan-Asian–inspired dishes, often featuring tofu. Stir-fries are ultra-fast to make and use only one or two pots, which is key for me when we're just trying to make it across the finish line. Also, you can throw in any veggies that are sitting in the fridge looking forlorn, or alternatively, you can make it from just about anything when you have almost no food left—good ol' carrots and cabbage are highly stir-fry-able. We especially like Garlic-Soy Tofu with Mushrooms and Napa Cabbage (page 197), Stir-Fried Peanut Noodles (page 203), and Miso Ramen (page 208).

Weekends, including Friday evenings, are unplanned. We graze on leftovers, see friends for a meal in or out, make burgers, or put out a table of snacks, like hummus, cut raw veggies, smoked tofu, olives, crackers, and fermented grapes (wine. I'm talking about wine). We usually make brunch at least once. I end the weekend feeling refreshed and ready to tackle another week, starting with the on-ramp easy Monday pasta meal.

Although some weeks call for rearranging or deviating from the themes, I find this loose plan incredibly helpful. There is some variety naturally built into each week. I can stop in at the produce market without a list and pick up a few things by running through my mental list of categories: pasta, bowls, one-pot meals, and/or stir-fries. I can plan a little without needing to actually sit down to plan. And most importantly, it requires much less ongoing organizational effort.

Choose Your Own Adventure

If these specific themes don't suit your eating preferences but you'd still like to try cooking by theme, here's what I suggest you do:

1. Consider which days and meals you'd benefit from having themes (I have dinner themes for Monday through Thursday, but there's no reason you can't celebrate sandwiches on Mondays at lunchtime).

2. Make a list of your family's favourite meals, recipes, cuisines (e.g., Mexican, Indian), and themes (e.g., breakfast for dinner, oven bakes). Also include foods you'd like to eat weekly, such as beans, tofu, or quinoa.

3. See what themes are emerging from your list. How can they be organized into workable categories? Consider whether you want to go narrow (e.g., burger night) or broad (e.g., handhelds night) and what, in practice, you'd include in each category.

4. Write out your themes with a list of example meals and post the plan somewhere you'll see it daily (for me, this is the fridge door).

5. Try out your themes for a week or two, and then reflect on how they're working. Does anything need to be tweaked to make it work better for you?

All right, so maybe you don't want to cook by themes. I accept that, proselytize as I may, not everyone is going to be as stoked as I am about cooking this way. At the very least, I encourage you to have some sort of plan in place that works for you, to minimize the anxiety that comes along with constantly wondering what's for dinner. Maybe you plan each meal with specificity each week or month (I bow down to your organizational skills). Maybe a big meal-prep day on Sunday makes your week run more smoothly. Maybe you are one of those rare specimens who can just contentedly wing it each day as long as you have groceries. Experiment until you find a strategy that feels right for you. However you approach your week, the family-friendly, real-world-tested recipes in this book can help you get a delicious and nutritious meal on the table with ease.

My Family's Food Staples

Are you as fascinated as I am by what groceries other people buy? I can be in a grocery store and be fairly disinterested in what's on the shelves beyond what I'm buying for myself. But the second those same groceries are collected in someone's basket or on the conveyor belt in front of me at checkout, I'm riveted. Suddenly those groceries tell a story, offering an intimate peek into someone's life. I find myself imagining how this stranger might cook and eat, and by extension, live. There is something humanizing about picturing someone at home, heating up a can of soup in their kitchen or cutting up fruit for their kids or gamely cooking something complicated from scratch. Despite our many differences, we all cut our broccoli one stalk at a time.

By sharing what's in my fridge and pantry, I'm not providing you with a shopping list. Instead, it's a peek into my grocery cart, as it were. So much of what I'm trying to do with *The Vegan Family Cookbook* is to get away from contextless recipes, to show how cooking and food preparation fit into a real life. To do that, you need to see what I'm working with.

We are a mostly gluten-free family, because one of my children doesn't tolerate gluten well, and it's easiest to simply cook gluten-free for all. All our staples, and the recipes in this book, happen to be gluten-free—but, of course, you can use wheat-based products (including flours) instead, if you'd like.

Grains and Starches

Grains and starches form the base of most of our meals. My active kids especially eat large servings of these energy-giving foods. We buy 25-lb (11.5 kg) bags of oats from our local food co-op every three months or so and eat them every day in the form of Hands-Off Creamy Oatmeal (page 56), Oat Waffles (page 59), and Chunky Oil-Free Granola (page 52). We also eat noodles, rice, and potatoes once or twice every week.

- Bread
- Cereal (we like Nature's Path brand)
- Flour (all-purpose; we like Bob's Red Mill gluten-free all-purpose baking flour)
- Noodles (ramen, rice; for stir-fries, soups)
- Oats (for oatmeal, granola, pancakes, waffles, cookies)
- Pasta
- Polenta
- Potatoes (yellow, russet)
- Quinoa or millet (for bowls, salads)
- Rice (brown jasmine; for bowls, stir-fries, nori rolls)
- Sweet potatoes

Legumes

Protein- and iron-rich legumes are essentially what we eat where others might eat meat. Legumes are filling and nutritious and, with just a little seasoning, absolutely delicious. Most food cultures around the world—from Indian to Ethiopian to Mexican—include legumes as a staple food. I typically stick to a few favourite types of beans and lentils and buy them dried.

- Black beans (for rice and beans, soups, tacos, bowls)
- Cannellini beans (for sauces, dips, soups, bowls, pasta)
- Chickpea flour (for crepes, waffles)
- Chickpeas (for hummus, curries, chickpea salad sandwiches, bowls)
- French lentils (for soups, pasta, stews, curries)
- Pinto beans (for rice and beans, tacos, bowls, pasta)
- Red lentils (for soups, curries)
- Tofu (for stir-fries, soups, curries, sandwiches)

Vegetables

We eat lots of vegetables every day, and in different forms. The kids favour snacking on raw veggies, like bell pepper, cucumber, and carrot. Arden and I enjoy salads with our meals most days. I include vegetables, generally cooked, with our dinner—always. We all like our green smoothies. In the warmer months, we get many of our veggies from our garden; kale is my all-time favourite thing to grow. Besides what's on the list below, we also enjoy whatever we can get our hands on (or grow) seasonally, such as radishes in the spring and kabocha squash in the autumn.

- Avocado
- Bell peppers (green for cooking; red, orange, yellow for snacking)
- Broccoli
- Bok choy
- Cabbage (red, green, napa)
- Carrots
- Cauliflower
- Corn (frozen)
- Cucumber
- Kale
- Lettuce (leaf, romaine)
- Mushrooms
- Onions (red, white, yellow, green)
- Peas (frozen)
- Tomatoes

Fruits

One of the best things about summer is the steady stream of ripe, seasonal fruits. We love gorging on whatever is at its peak and, right about the time we're getting sick of it, moving on to the next fruit that's suddenly everywhere, looking irresistible. Probably like most kids, mine can't seem to get enough of fruit, and they eat it all day long. We also keep big bags of organic fruit in the freezer for smoothies, oatmeal, and crumbles.

- Apples
- Apricots
- Bananas
- Berries (frozen)
- Blackberries
- Blueberries
- Cherries
- Figs
- Grapes
- Mango (fresh or frozen)
- Nectarines
- Oranges
- Peaches
- Pears

- Persimmons
- Plums
- Raspberries
- Strawberries
- Watermelon

Sauces, Spreads, and Seasonings

Sauces, spreads, and seasonings are how we make our foundational whole plant foods more delicious. We use these ingredients at pretty much every meal. I don't feel badly about including some processed foods as accents to our meals, because they make life easier and more delicious, and because my belief is that healthy diets can include small amounts of convenience foods. Besides, I would be sad without my vegan mayo, and that can't be healthy.

- Citrus fruit: lemons and limes
- Dijon mustard (for sandwiches, dressings)
- Dried herbs and spices: bay leaves, cardamom, cinnamon, coriander, cumin (ground and seeds), fennel seeds, garlic powder, mustard seeds, onion powder, oregano, paprika (smoked and sweet), sage (essential for Thanksgiving/Christmas meals), thyme, turmeric
- Fresh herbs: basil, cilantro, parsley, dill, chives, rosemary
- Garlic
- Hot sauces
- Ketchup (purchased under duress for my kids)
- Maple syrup (we use pure)
- Marinara or passata sauce
- Miso (for sauces, soups, pestos, hot drinks; we like Hikari Miso brand white, a.k.a. "white type," miso)
- Natural peanut butter (for toast, oatmeal, smoothies, peanut sauces, baked goods)
- Nutritional yeast
- Peppercorns
- Quality iodized salt and finishing salts
- Red pepper flakes
- Sesame oil
- Soy sauce or tamari
- Tahini (for hummus, sauces, dressings, granola, baked goods)
- Vanilla extract (we use pure)
- Vinegars: apple cider, balsamic, red wine, rice, white

- Vegan butter (we like Earth Balance brand)
- Vegan mayo (we like Vegenaise brand)

A Note on Spices

I try to restrain myself when it comes to buying spices. I prefer having a small collection of spices and dried herbs that I really like and know how to use. Old spices lose their flavour; very old spices can muddy the taste of whatever you're cooking. This is why you'll see some repetition in what spices I use.

If you're averse to any of the seasonings I incorporate in the *The Vegan Family Cookbook* recipes, skip them, or perhaps replace them with something you prefer. If you're still learning what you love, smell spices and consider how their aroma appeals to you. Cook with them and see if you can identify the flavour they impart, and reflect on how much you like it. Remember, if what you cook tastes good to *you*, it's a good dish.

Nuts and Seeds

Nuts and seeds are so nutritious, and they're a delicious way to add unprocessed fats to our diet. We use them in smoothies, oatmeal, pestos, and sauces, and as a topping for bowls, stir-fries, and other meals. In addition to these staples, we also mix things up by rotating through some other nuts, like pistachios, macadamias, and tamari- or lemon-roasted almonds.

- Cashews
- Chia seeds
- Flax seeds
- Hemp seeds
- Pumpkin seeds
- Sesame seeds (toasted)
- Walnuts

Snacks and Sweets

I tease my kids for eating six meals a day: breakfast, morning snack, lunch, afternoon snack, dinner, and evening snack. They're always eating! In addition to the foods listed elsewhere in this section (like fruit, hummus, and smoothies), I make sure to have theses items on hand for snacks and sweets:

- Dark chocolate
- Dried fruit (e.g., mango, apricots, raisins)
- Medjool dates

- Popping corn
- Whole grain crackers
- Vegan ice cream (not an everyday food)

Beverages

For the most part, we drink good ol' tap water, using a filter to remove chlorine. Arden and I also have our daily coffee and tea respectively. We don't always have juice on hand for the kids, but we do rotate it through fairly regularly—I like including a small glass of vitamin-C-rich orange juice with their meals sometimes to boost iron absorption, or we'll try a different juice to mix it up.

- Coffee
- Dried herbs for tea (lemon balm, mint, holy basil)
- Homemade Chocolate Milk (page 48)
- Loose leaf black and green tea
- Mineral water (great source of calcium and magnesium, and so tasty!)
- Orange juice
- Tap water
- Unsweetened soy milk

Other

There are a few more staples that you'll almost always find in our cupboards that didn't fit in any of the sections above:

- Almond flour
- Avocado oil
- Baking powder
- Baking soda
- Cocoa powder
- Coconut milk
- Cornstarch
- Dill pickles
- Extra virgin olive oil
- Nori sheets
- Sauerkraut

Some of My Indispensable Tools

There are a few food preparation tools I reach for again and again, and that make it easier and more pleasant for me to be in the kitchen. The key is zeroing in on which tools are genuinely helpful and which just add clutter to your space. Of course, we all have our preferences. I find fruit slicers clunky to use, unwieldy to store, and annoying to clean, while others swear by them. Meanwhile, I can't believe there's a resale market for pressure cookers—who could possibly not love this magical device?! Here's a list of some of the tools I use often.

A large knife. One good-quality knife is all you need. For many years, I used an 8-inch (20 cm) chef's knife. Now I use a 7-inch (18 cm) santoku knife. Both are great. Learn how to hold it properly, with your index finger getting cozy with the blade for better control and more leverage, to make chopping veggies and other ingredients quick and relatively easy.

A large cutting board. I like having a large cutting board so I'm not feeling crowded on a small surface. Actually, I have a few cutting boards—a large one for just about everything, including stinky onions and garlic, a smaller one for only fruit, and a long one for only bread—but I only consider the large one strictly essential. If I were being banished to a desert island (unlikely, but it's good to plan ahead), it's the only one I'd pack.

A citrus squeezer. Lemons and limes make food taste so much better, and having a citrus squeezer on hand can make the difference between my using fresh citrus or not. Citrus squeezers catch the seeds and get every drop out of the citrus, and they do it in seconds. I use mine all the time.

A mandoline. This is probably only necessary if you regularly eat slaws, which I do. Cabbage thinly shaved on a mandoline is more tender and flavourful than what most of us can pull off with a knife—it better absorbs dressing and is more pleasant to chew. I also like shaving other raw dense veggies, like fennel, radishes, and sunchokes, to lighten them up for a change. Everyone knows radishes can be way too serious.

Cast iron skillets. I grew up using cast iron skillets and I love them. They are mildly non-stick, so they work well for "sticky" things like pancakes. However, unlike with synthetically non-stick skillets, food can stick to them enough to brown or even blacken, when that's what you're going for. I have 9-inch (23 cm) and 12-inch (30 cm) cast iron skillets and they live on my stove because I use them daily.

A wooden spatula. If you're using cast iron, it's worthwhile having a wooden cooking utensil or two with a square edge, which is gentler on cast iron's finish than metal. Square edges, as opposed to round, are ideal for easily scraping and lifting food.

Saucepans with glass lids. I have three heavy-bottomed saucepans of varying sizes, each with well-fitting glass lids. I use them daily for cooking grains, steaming vegetables, and other smaller-scale cookery. I like that I can see at a glance what's happening with the food and whether it's approaching being done.

A large pot. Anyone eating a plant-based diet is probably going to be cooking their fair share of soups, stews, curries, and pastas. Large pots are essential for this. My large pot also has a glass lid—again, so handy for peeking at simmering food to see how it's coming along.

Steaming basket. I prefer steaming veggies to boiling them so as not to lose so many of the water-soluble vitamins in the cooking water. Steamed veggies are soft and moist, which has its place for all of us but is especially palatable to kids.

A high-speed blender. These high-wattage blenders make extra-creamy sauces, soups, and smoothies. Yes, they are expensive. For us, the investment has been well worth it. We've been using a Blendtec since 2010 and I highly recommend it.

A food processor. Maybe not necessary if you already have a blender. But we use our food processor for all manner of thicker mixtures, including oat balls, pesto, veggie burgers, "nice cream" (frozen bananas blitzed to a soft-serve-like texture), dairy-free Parmesan-style topping, and creamy oil-free hummus. I also use it when I need to chop large quantities of veggies—a few pulses, and onions are finely chopped.

An electric pressure cooker. I resisted buying one for the longest time. Now, I use it at least weekly and love having it. It makes beans and split lentils extra creamy, and once the food is in, it requires zero monitoring, which I appreciate during this busy season of my life. It can also make hands-off quick polenta!

A toaster. Does anyone *not* have a toaster? Toasting bread and putting stuff on it is the easiest meal in the world.

Cooking—with or without Recipes

Recipes have a role: sometimes it can be fun to learn to make a totally new dish, and there's no denying that recipes are the best way to communicate with others how to replicate a dish. But I think we also have to recognize that recipes are merely one tool we can use, and that when we do use them, it's not actually against the rules to approach them more as guidelines than as rigid instructions.

Recipes with measurements are a relatively modern phenomenon. Once upon a time, people learned to cook by watching others, and by tasting. Early recipes were more like loose instructions written in brief paragraphs. For example, take this recipe for wild boar from the fourth or fifth century AD:

> Wild boar is prepared thus: it is cleaned; sprinkled with salt and crushed cumin and thus left. The next day it is put into the oven; when done season with crushed pepper. A sauce for boar: honey broth, reduced wine, raisin wine.[2]

Interesting, right? I prefer my wild boar alive, so I'd try this one with tofu, but the concept of simply adding some unknown quantities of ingredients and cooking at an unspecified temperature until "done" feels freeing to me.

Following recipes closely is a great way to learn to cook, but once we're ready to leave the nest, it makes sense to get a little experimental. Why? Because cooking without recipes saves time, is more flexible, and empowers us to be more confident, resourceful cooks. No taking time to measure things out or dirtying up measuring utensils. No last-minute dash to the store for a zucchini when you only have a green bell pepper, or conversely, no zucchini rotting in the fridge because none of our recipes call for it. No more unsatisfying results because your tahini was thicker than the recipe creator's. We learn to really taste food, to identify for ourselves when something is delicious and why, and we enjoy cooking more because it's a creative activity rather than a chore.

Although this book contains recipes, know that they are amalgams of how I make our family's favourite foods most of the time. But I'll often add a little of this, or skip a little of that, based on what ingredients we have on hand or how I'm feeling inspired in the moment. I encourage you to do the same. Recipes can be approached as guidelines, to be played with to suit your own preferences.

The worst that can happen is that you get a mediocre meal once in a while. On the bright side, you'll have learned something new, and next time you'll have a better sense of how to adapt a recipe to suit you. Accept that the road to becoming a more versatile and intuitive cook is paved with mistakes, and we've all been there.

Ultimately, a dish is good if it tastes good to *you*. There are infinite ways to make even the simplest things, like vinaigrette. Relationships have probably ended over disputes about how to make hummus. Food is like music, art, and books: if you like it, it's good. If you don't like it, it's not for you and that's okay. Taste food you've cooked and answer the simple question "Does this taste good to me?" It the answer is no, it can sometimes take a little more experience to answer the follow-up question "What can I do to improve that?" But even so, your ability to answer this for yourself depends on *your* experience, not someone else's. Learn ideas and techniques from others, then have confidence to apply them to your own cooking in a way that suits you.

Making friends with cooking

Sometimes it's going to feel like a chore to cook dinner. We're doing it every day, often feeding others, cleaning up, too, and it starts all over again the next day. This is a lot. People write to me to ask how I find the motivation to do it day in and day out. The truth is, in the beginning, I wasn't all that motivated. Instead, I committed to cooking each day out of necessity. I went into the kitchen and made dinner because it needed to be done. It didn't filter through my brain as a choice, and so motivation didn't need to come into play. But a funny thing happened along the way: I came to really, genuinely love being in the kitchen.

At dinnertime, I turn on beautiful music, put on an apron if I'm cooking something that splatters, sometimes pour a small glass of wine, and get to work. I've been doing this every weekday for years and it has become a ritual that anchors my day. I always have a bit of a plan (see What's for Dinner, page 10), so I'm not dealing with that dreaded mental barrier of wondering what the heck to make. I don't cook meals that take longer than 30 or maybe 45 minutes, eliminating the sense of exhaustion that comes from an ambitious kitchen project. I find enormous satisfaction in putting together a meal, creatively moving nutritious ingredients through our kitchen, always a little differently as the seasons and our tastes change. It's like a puzzle—a delicious puzzle that you can eat.

I can honestly say now that I love cooking—not just fun cooking projects once in a while but the daily cycle of putting meals together for my family. This is a learned attitude. By accepting it as a necessity, I started doing it without resistance. By doing it, I became better at it. Now that I have the skills to manage a high-volume kitchen, I enjoy doing it—after all, it's gratifying to do things we're skilled at. Make friends with cooking and you'll see that it can actually be a pretty decent friend. And if you still don't feel like making dinner? That's what hummus is for.

Flavour fundamentals: making food delicious

When you're experimenting with modifying recipes, putting together a plate of leftovers, or simply freestyling a meal, it can help to have a basic understanding of how to make food taste good. This is especially true with animal-free cooking—we need to understand the role that meat and dairy play in dishes so we can replicate that when using plant-based ingredients or cooking techniques.

At the same time, I'm constantly trying to strike a balance between flavour and nutrition. Sure, we could douse everything we cook in oil and salt, and it would be delicious, but then we wouldn't be feeling our best now or in the future, and cooking is as much about nourishment as it is flavour. We have to find the sweet spot. (Sorry, I'm a mom—I can't help but bring a health lecture to this discussion on flavour.)

These flavour principles are another mental checklist I go through when preparing meals:

Salt

Apparently, salt is the most-used seasoning in the world. Is anyone surprised? Salt—which is a mineral rather than a spice—doesn't so much contribute its own flavour as it does enhance the flavours of whatever you're cooking. I'm constantly amazed by how the simple addition of salt can transform a bland-tasting dish into something complex, flavourful, and irresistible.

Still, many of us try to minimize our salt intake for good cardiovascular and bone health—although, happily, some sodium in our diets is essential. According to Health Canada, 1 tsp (5 mL) of fine-grain salt contains about 2300 milligrams (mg) of sodium. Children aged 1 to 3 years should get between 1000 and 1500 mg of sodium per day. For children aged 4 to 8, it's 1200 mg to 1900 mg. Teens and adults should aim for 1500 mg to 2200 mg and 2300 mg respectively. Older adults need a little less.[3]

Fortunately, with training, our taste buds can adjust to find these modest quantities of salt satisfying. The best way to do this is by cooking for ourselves at home, keeping salt-added packaged and takeout foods to a minimum. I find that food cooked at restaurants—which I used to love—almost always tastes too salty to me now. Another hack to minimize salt without compromising flavour is to intentionally under-salt food while cooking, and then shake on a little salt at the table. When salt hits our taste receptors directly, rather than being dissolved in a dish, we perceive food as being saltier.

When I'm cooking, I use salt to enhance flavour without going overboard. In practice, this means I limit added salt to no more than ¼ tsp (1 mL) per adult serving. Instead of using a pinch of salt here and there and losing track, I keep a ¼ tsp (1 mL) measure in my salt dish so I know exactly how much I'm adding.

Pepper

Salt's trusty sidekick, black pepper, is the most-used spice in the world (only because salt technically isn't a spice so can't take that honour). Assuming everyone in the world is on to something, let's use black pepper liberally. Pepper added early in cooking contributes a little tolerable heat and extra warming body to the final dish. Pepper fresh cracked at the table contributes a lovely fragrance and more pungent heat. There's no need to use pre-ground peppercorns, which rapidly lose their flavour, when grinders are so readily available.

Acidity

Adding a little something sour to a dish can create complexity and interest. Acidic ingredients especially balance nicely with fatty ingredients, by cutting the richness a little, and with sweet ingredients—hello, sweet-and-sour sauce. Not every component of a meal needs to have acidity. We can simply add a little something on the plate to provide contrast and balance—a creamy pasta is made more satisfying when served with a vinaigrette-dressed salad, for example. There are many sour ingredients to choose from: all manner of vinegars; citrus fruits, like lemons, limes, and even grapefruits; tomatoes; other fruits and veggies, including cranberries, rhubarb, and pomegranate; pickled foods, like dill pickles and quick-pickled cabbage or onion; and fermented foods, like sauerkraut, kimchi, miso, and unsweetened coconut yogurt.

Have you ever had genmai tea, maybe at a sushi restaurant? It's green tea with toasted brown rice. Green tea has modest amounts of glutamate, and toasting the brown rice releases glutamate. You may not have realized you were drinking a classic umami love story.

Umami

Glutamate is an amino acid that's especially prevalent in meats and dairy (and, interestingly, breastmilk). Foods containing glutamate trigger our umami, or savoury, taste receptors. You can't exactly taste umami, but you will likely notice its presence or absence by how satisfying a meal feels to you.

When cooking without glutamate-rich meats and dairy, then, it helps to make an effort to include glutamate-rich ingredients from plant sources. These include mushrooms, tomatoes, walnuts, and nutritional yeast (find this healthful and delicious deactivated yeast in the natural foods section of most well-stocked grocery stores). Potatoes, broccoli, green peas, corn, and napa cabbage all also naturally contain modest amounts of glutamate.

The glutamate available in plant-based foods can also be increased during preparation; fermenting and browning food increases glutamate by freeing it from proteins. Think of familiar fermented foods like soy sauce, miso, wine, beer, and aged vinegars (e.g., balsamic)—they taste particularly rich and delicious to us. Also consider how cooking techniques like roasting, grilling, searing, and toasting can significantly enhance a food's crave-worthiness. Eating roasted cauliflower is a totally different experience from eating it steamed.

Browning

Food browns when cooked in the absence of moisture because of the Maillard reaction, which is the process by which amino acids (including, but not limited to, glutamate) react with sugars to create flavour compounds. Use this to your flavour advantage by toasting bread, tortillas, nuts, and seeds; roasting potatoes, beets, carrots, asparagus, cauliflower, fennel bulbs, tomatoes, garlic, and onions; searing tofu, mushrooms, corn, Brussels sprouts, and broccoli; frying spices until they turn a shade darker; and just generally browning anything that seems good to you. Including even just one browned ingredient in a dish—such as toasted pumpkin seeds on your tacos or pan-fried fennel seeds in your soup—can seriously elevate it.

Fat

Some fat is important not only for nutrition but also for food enjoyment—it adds a uniquely rich and satisfying mouthfeel to our food. Fat can also make foods crispy or, conversely, creamy, both of which are universally pleasing textures. And the flavour of many herbs and spices is fat-soluble, so when they're toasted in a little oil, more of their flavour compounds will be released into your dish.

Even so-called lean meats and animal products, like skinless chicken breasts and eggs, contain significantly more fat than plant-based foods. When cooking plant-based meals, then, it helps to add some of that fat back in via healthy fats from nuts, seeds, extra virgin olive oil, coconut milk, tahini, nut-based cream sauces, and so on. Your meals will be more delicious, and you will leave the table feeling more satisfied.

On the other hand, concentrated fats, like oil and coconut milk, can be easy to overdo. We don't need to sauté an onion in spoonfuls of oil when one will do. One way to get the most of concentrated fats is to add them at the end of cooking, when their silky body won't be degraded—adding coconut milk at or near the end of cooking preserves more of its tongue-coating richness. A little drizzle of olive oil on a bowl of soup transforms its mouthfeel and flavour, while that same oil would just have got lost had it been added earlier.

Texture

When I started cooking for myself, I relied on many one-pot meals, such as chilis, soups, and curries. These meals are easy to make and deliver big on taste, and are staples in most plant-based diets. But despite these foods tasting delicious, I found myself tiring of them and not really understanding why—It tastes good, so why am I shuddering at the thought of heating up those leftovers? It took me many years to realize I was missing one crucial factor: texture.

Meat provides something we can sink our teeth into, which feels so satisfying. When cooking plant-based, it helps to include different textures to help recreate this satisfying feeling. Creating textural contrast is as simple as pairing a one-pot meal with some chewy bread or a crisp salad, or topping our bowls with some crunchy nuts and seeds. It's also one reason noodles are so universally popular—they're chewy and a delight to eat.

Moisture

It's not unusual to hear people self-identify as sauce lovers (myself included). In addition to contributing flavour, sauces provide moisture, which feels good in our mouths. But it's not always necessary to use a complicated sauce to achieve this. A drizzle of olive oil and a squeeze of lemon juice, for example, can significantly enhance a dish, not only by providing fat and acid but by introducing moisture.

One-pot meals don't really need any help in this department, because they're inherently saucy. But when preparing most other meals—including pasta, bowls, stir-fries, sandwiches, crepes, and so forth—I consider whether there is enough moisture. A little sauce on a quinoa-based bowl can transform something you're choking down into something crave-worthy. A noodle stir-fry can go from good to great with an extra drizzle of soy sauce and a squeeze of lime juice at the table. A creamy pasta sauce that's too thick can feel sticky in your mouth—thin it out with a little water and all will be right with the world.

Take stock, then cook

I feel like I'm in a constant dance between filling up our fridge with food to eat and eating through the food while it's still at its best. The only thing more satisfying than a fridge filled with yummy meals and prepped ingredients is, later, a nearly empty fridge because we haven't let anything go to waste. Then the cycle begins again.

It requires a little skill to use and repurpose the food we have in our fridges and pantries, but most of all it requires our attention—and our intention. It's important to me to do my best to minimize food waste. I also feel more relaxed and in control of my space when I'm not swimming in half-used condiments, containers, bags, and cans.

If this is you too, may I suggest making it a habit to regularly take stock of what you already have before deciding on a meal. Try to incorporate the most perishable items today or tomorrow. At lunchtime, if there's just a single portion of quinoa leftover, I might base my meal around that—maybe by sautéing some beans, veggies, and garlic to scoop on top. If I'm planning to make pasta for dinner, I'll pull out the third of a jar of tomato sauce and the mushrooms that aren't getting any juicier and try to incorporate those into the pasta. (Most of the times I cook rosé sauce, it was borne of the happy accident of having some form of tomato that needed using.) I apply this thinking to the pantry, too: I made teff pancakes one morning, for example, solely because some teff grains had been languishing in the cupboards for months. (I blended the teff with water, cinnamon, and baking powder; the pancakes were delicious.) Taking stock of what we have and being deliberate about moving food through our kitchens helps us become more creative cooks.

I often start a meal by pulling out anything I think I might use. I don't necessarily use it all, but having it in front of me helps me consider how the ingredients might work together. Anything that doesn't get used will be put away, and having handled it, it'll be top of mind (and front of fridge) next time. These small habits and attitude adjustments have helped dramatically cut down on the food that goes to waste in our kitchen.

Creating nutritionally balanced meals

When I'm thinking about what to cook, I also mentally filter my choices through a few basic nutrition principles. I want our meals to be tasty and practical but also nutritionally balanced. Food is pleasure and connection; it is also fuel and nourishment.

This is absolutely not everything you need to know to be healthy as a plant-based eater. I encourage you to use an evidence-based resource like www.veganhealth.org or consult with a registered dietitian to learn more about eating well for optimum health and to ensure you're appropriately supplementing your diet.

Here are a few principles I consider when creating balanced meals, which you'll see reflected in the recipes throughout *The Vegan Family Cookbook*.

Include legumes a few times a day. I try to include legumes in almost every lunch and dinner. Legumes are a class of protein-rich plants that includes beans, lentils, chickpeas, peas, and derivatives like hummus, tofu, soy milk, and peanut butter. Technically, the part that we eat is the plants' seeds, which I suppose explains why legumes are such concentrated sources of nutrients:

they're rich in protein (including the amino acid lysine, which is especially important for vegans), fibre, antioxidants, iron, zinc, and a slew of other minerals and vitamins. They contain no saturated fat. As the mature seeds of plants, they count toward our daily vegetable servings.

I don't think I'll ever get too excited about cauliflower burgers or jackfruit tacos. Why not? Because all I can see is a missed opportunity to use legumes. Instead of battering cauliflower or shredding jackfruit, I'm using that time to make bean-based burger patties or seasoning beans for tacos.

Choose mostly whole grains. I'm sure you've gotten the memo by now that whole grains contain more nutrients than their refined counterparts. They are also digested more slowly, helping stabilize blood sugar and stave off hunger. In general, the closer a grain is to its intact state, the better—for example, brown rice is a little better than brown rice flour—because nutrients degrade at each processing step. As a family, we love brown jasmine rice, and I use rolled oats where I can as a base for pancakes, waffles, and even cookies. That said, we do love our noodles, too.

Consume as many dark leafy greens as possible. Dark leafy greens, like kale, chard, and lettuces, are ridiculously nutrient-dense. These greens are rich in several vitamins and minerals important for plant-based eaters: the vitamin A precursor beta carotene (you just can't see the orange beneath all that green), vitamin K, calcium, and vitamin C (which boosts iron absorption).

Choose a variety of colours and plant foods. Different colours signal the presence of different phytochemicals, all of which are uniquely useful to our bodies. Eating a variety of red, orange, yellow, green, blue, and purple fruits and vegetables not only looks beautiful, it can protect us from inflammation and chronic diseases. And research shows that people who consume more than 30 types of plants each week have much more diverse microbiomes (i.e., the bugs in our guts that have an enormous impact on our health) than people who eat fewer than 10.[5]

Plant-Loving Pintos

Legumes are extremely environmentally friendly: they're drought-tolerant crops that improve soil health by adding fertilizing nitrogen, while also removing greenhouse gases from the air. Pretty impressive!

The Food and Agriculture Organization of the United Nations promotes the consumption of legumes globally not only for their significant nutritional benefits but because of the important role they play in improving the sustainability of agricultural systems and, in turn, food security.[4]

Eat cruciferous vegetables often. Cruciferous vegetables, including broccoli, cauliflower, cabbage, and my BFF, kale, may be especially health-promoting. Research has shown that this class of sulphur-containing vegetables may protect against cancer,[6] promote heart health,[7] help manage type-2 diabetes,[8] promote cognitive health,[9] protect against sun damage,[10] and even improve autism symptoms.[11] Cruciferous veggies are some of my favourites to grow, because they're hardy and can be high-yielding—and it's such a pleasure to pick them fresh for each meal throughout the growing season. My annual garden is never without kale, arugula, watercress, and radishes.

Consume omega-3-rich foods every day. Omega-3 fats are essential for good health, and we must get them either from the foods we eat or from supplements. I make a point of including omega-rich flax, hemp, chia, and/or walnuts in our daily diet.

Include plenty of nuts and seeds. Nuts and seeds are a good source of healthy fats and protein, and many are also rich in the essential mineral zinc. Having a range of nuts and seeds on hand to stir into oatmeal, blend into sauces and smoothies, sprinkle on bowls, and snack on outright is an easy way to increase variety in our diets and boost nutrition.

Ensure a source of iodine. Decades ago, iodine deficiency was a major public health concern, until we started iodizing salt. However, in recent years, a trend away from using iodized table salt has resulted in a resurgence of iodine deficiency. I use good-quality iodized salt (Costco sells iodized Himalayan pink salt) for cooking and save the special salts for sprinkling on top of dishes, where the taste really comes through. We also regularly consume seaweed, another good source of iodine.

Don't skimp too much on fat. Fat is essential for the absorption of fat-soluble nutrients and to promote satiety (that feeling of fullness and satisfaction you get after eating). In addition to using foods like nuts, seeds, coconut milk, tahini, and peanut butter, I use a small amount of anti-inflammatory extra virgin olive oil to dress salads and gently sauté, avocado oil for higher heat roasting or sautéing, and sesame oil for its amazing flavour.

Why Do I Use Oil?

I often get asked about my use of oil, since some health experts promote oil-free diets. My position is that a moderate amount of oil can be part of a healthy diet for those of us who do not have a medical reason to eliminate it. Contrary to popular belief, oil does contain nutrients—olive oil, for example, is a source of vitamins E and K. Oil is also a convenient way of incorporating some fat in our diets, which is crucial for the absorption of fat-soluble vitamins A, D, E, and K. At the same time, a little oil goes a long way—it's calorie-dense and rich. I try to cook with just enough oil to boost nutrition and flavour, but not so much that we're not feeling our best. My recipes reflect my quest for this sweet spot.

Make room for "fun" foods. My food philosophy is that it's neither necessary nor practical to eat only the most nutritious foods 100 percent of the time. Sure, it's important to make mostly healthful food choices. But what really matters is our overall eating patterns, and maybe most of all, our stress-free relationship with food. We enjoy processed and convenience foods once in a while, too. Chopped and sautéed Beyond Meat sausage added to soup is to die for. And is it even summer without an occasional scoop of vegan ice cream?

Visual Appeal

When my little brother Jake was 15, he worked in a French restaurant where the chef would say, "The first bite is with the eyes." Ever since, my family—all of us appreciators of the joy of simple home-cooked meals—have often repeated this adage when we sit down to a meal together.

I take a moment to plate food in a visually appealing way, considering colours, arrangement, and garnishes. I'm not talking about sweating over an overly stylized art project—just simply taking a little care when putting meals together, rather than dumping it all on a plate.

How food tastes to us is influenced by our other senses and even our attitudes. When we sit down to a beautiful plate of food that we feel grateful for and excited to dig into, we will enjoy it that much more. The first bite is, indeed, with the eyes. Take a moment to create and enjoy this first "bite."

Breakfast and Brunch

Cooking for a family is a marathon, and pacing ourselves is essential. For me, this means that at breakfast and lunch on weekdays, I'm not going to spend too much time at the stove making large meals—I conserve that effort for our evening family meal. Otherwise, I know I will get burnt-out.

One of our top weekday breakfasts is Hands-Off Creamy Oatmeal (page 56). I like that I can get in plenty of omega-3-rich seeds and some satiating, protein-rich soy milk. Oats are also healthy, inexpensive, and environmentally friendly. We buy 25-lb (11.5 kg) paper bags of organic oats for about $30 every three months or so from our local food co-op. I also use these oats to make my Chunky Oil-Free Granola (page 52), which I've made so many times I could now do it with my eyes closed. I love the granola with Cardamom-Cinnamon Milk (page 48).

When Arden or I have a little extra time and energy in the morning, we make Blender Oat Pancakes (page 55) and Oat Waffles (page 59), which our kids love. Both recipes contain almost the same ingredients as our oatmeal but feel a bit more exciting. I suggest that any family with children (or waffle enthusiasts) invest in a waffle maker, because it's such an incredible tool for turning wholesome ingredients into delicious, kid-friendly meals. I find waffles totally undemanding to make because—once you're used to your waffle maker—you don't need to manage the temperature or monitor for doneness; simply pour in the batter, set a timer, and go do something else. I've included four waffle recipes in this chapter, which speaks to my love of them as a family food.

Most mornings Arden or I will make a smoothie, either as the main event or as a complement to what we're eating. Like oatmeal, smoothies are a great vehicle for flax, chia, and hemp seeds. Our two favourites are our everyday Big Green Smoothie (page 50) and, for upset tummies, the Immune-Boosting Mango Ginger Smoothie (page 50).

Eggs are a common breakfast and brunch food. While we don't eat them, we do invoke the spirit of eggs in our brunches using ingredients like chickpea flour and tofu. My heart-healthy Fried No-Egg Sandwich (page 62) has convinced people to swap out eggs permanently. We mark the start of many weekends with delicious Simple Scrambled Tofu (page 65) alongside vegan sausage, toast, roasted potatoes, salad, avocado, and/or tortillas. And if we have leftover roasted potatoes, Brunch Hash (page 66) with toasted fennel seeds is a major family favourite.

No-Strain Milk, Three Ways

Each recipe makes 2¾ cups (685 mL)

I'm so happy to live in a time and place where a wide variety of plant-based milks is available in grocery stores. We regularly purchase these milks, especially soy milk for our kids because of its solid protein and fat content. But to my tastes, nothing beats the body, flavour, and nutrition of simple, whole ingredients blended at home.

I rely on a combination of cashews and hemp seeds for most homemade milks. Cashews create a neutral-sweet base, while hemp seeds contribute a boost of nutrition. As a glorious bonus, cashews and hemp seeds are both quite soft, so they blend more easily than other nuts and seeds and don't really need straining before using. However, if your blender isn't very powerful, you may find it works best to use hot water instead of cold, or even to soak the nuts and seeds for 30 minutes or so (just put all the ingredients in the blender and allow to sit).

These milks have no stabilizers, so they will separate when stored in the fridge. Simply shake before using. Use within 4 to 5 days.

All-Purpose Milk

This basic milk can swap for an animal-based or other plant-based milk in virtually any scenario. Use it for baking muffins and quick breads, in place of water to splash into pastas or soups that need thinning, and for pouring over cereal and into hot drinks.

1. Put all the ingredients in a blender, adding the water last, and blend on the highest setting until very smooth, 90 seconds to 5 minutes, depending on the strength of your blender. Pause if the blender starts to feel hot.

¼ cup (60 mL) cashews

1 Tbsp (15 mL) hemp seeds

1 Tbsp (15 mL) pure maple syrup (optional)

Pinch of salt

2½ cups (625 mL) water

recipe continues

Cardamom-Cinnamon Milk

This is the milk I make most often. I love the subtle flavour the spices add to the milk, which also masks the slightly grassy tones of the hemp seeds. It pairs naturally with oats, granola, and tea, which are the main things we use milk for in our house. I also splash it into curries and other dishes to thin them out while adding a little body, where a subtle hint of these warming spices is fitting. I use cardamom pods because they have a stronger flavour than the pre-ground version, which quickly degrades. If using ground cardamom, how much you need will depend on how fresh the spice is.

1. Put all the ingredients in a blender, adding the water last, and blend on the highest setting until very smooth, 90 seconds to 5 minutes, depending on the strength of your blender. Pause if the blender starts to feel hot.

¼ cup (60 mL) cashews

1 Tbsp (15 mL) hemp seeds

1 Tbsp (15 mL) pure maple syrup (optional)

2 green cardamom pods, seeds extracted and ground, or ⅛ tsp (0.5 mL) ground cardamom, plus more to taste

¼ tsp (1 mL) cinnamon

Pinch of salt

2½ cups (625 mL) water

Chocolate Milk

Who doesn't love chocolate milk? This version is sweet and chocolatey enough for kids but also complex enough for grown-up palates. I often heat this milk in a saucepan to make hot chocolate, especially after chilly outdoor winter activities.

1. Put all the ingredients in a blender, adding the water last, and blend on the highest setting until very smooth, 90 seconds to 5 minutes, depending on the strength of your blender. Pause if the blender starts to feel hot.

¼ cup (60 mL) cashews

1 Tbsp (15 mL) hemp seeds

1½ Tbsp (22 mL) cocoa powder

2 to 3 Tbsp (30 to 45 mL) pure maple syrup, to taste

Pinch of salt

2½ cups (625 mL) water

Variation

Hot chocolate: Pour the chocolate milk into a saucepan and set over medium heat until steaming hot, stirring constantly.

Big Green Smoothie

Serves 1 to 2

I'm not exaggerating when I say Arden and I have made this smoothie a thousand times. From our busy law-student days to the stupor of new parenthood, this smoothie has been our vehicle for ensuring we're eating the foods that keep us functioning: flax seeds (for the omegas), kale (for the sulforaphane), berries (for the antioxidants), and soy milk (for the protein and heart-healthy fat).

1. Combine all the ingredients in a blender in the order listed. Blend until very smooth, 60 to 90 seconds.

1 banana

2 Tbsp (30 mL) flax seeds

2 to 3 kale leaves, tough stem ends snapped off

1 heaping cup (275 mL) frozen mixed berries

1 cup (250 mL) soy milk or other plant-based milk

1 cup (250 mL) water

Immune-Boosting Mango Ginger Smoothie

Serves 1

When one of us isn't feeling well, I turn to this tummy-soothing mango ginger smoothie. Bananas contain prebiotic fibre, which improves gut function—and did you know that the majority of our immune cells are in our gut? Mango is rich in vitamins A and C, both of which support immune function. Powerhouse ginger is anti-inflammatory, anti-viral, and anti-microbial, and can relieve nausea. Hemp seeds are rich in immune-supporting zinc.

1. Combine all the ingredients in a blender in the order listed. Blend until very smooth, 60 to 90 seconds.

1 ripe banana

1½ cups (375 mL) frozen mango

Grape-sized piece of ginger, peeled

1 Tbsp (15 mL) hemp seeds

1 cup (250 mL) water

Tip
To peel ginger, use the edge of a spoon for easy peeling with minimal wastage.

Berry Chia Sauce

Makes 2 to 2½ cups

This simple sauce is my favourite way to eat berries in the winter, when we're missing the smorgasbord of summer fruits. (I like to use mixed berries or wild blueberries.) Fresh from the pot, the warm sauce makes a great topping for oatmeal, pancakes, and waffles. Any leftovers that you refrigerate will thicken up and can be used more like jam.

1. Put the berries and water in a medium saucepan. Cook over medium heat, covered, until the berries are thawed and start to release some liquid.

2. Sprinkle in the chia seeds, then stir quickly so they don't clump. Simmer for 5 to 10 more minutes, uncovered, to soften the berries and thicken the sauce, mashing up the berries a little against the side of the pot.

3. Serve warm or cold. Refrigerate any leftovers in an airtight container for up to 4 days.

3 cups (750 mL) frozen berries of your choice

1 Tbsp (15 mL) water

1 Tbsp (15 mL) chia seeds

Vanilla Chia Breakfast Pudding

Serves 2 to 3

This is a filling and portable breakfast that many kids (and adults!) really like. I find it decadent, almost like eating dessert for breakfast. The chia seeds take a while to gel in this form, so make the pudding the night before. I use tahini in this recipe for a boost of nutrition—it contains a long list of vitamins and minerals, including iron and calcium.

1. Put all the ingredients in an airtight jar or storage container and mix well. After 15 minutes, mix again and then refrigerate overnight. Enjoy within 4 to 5 days.

1½ cups (375 mL) plant-based milk

¼ cup (60 mL) chia seeds

2 Tbsp (30 mL) tahini

1 to 2 Tbsp (15 to 30 mL) pure maple syrup, to taste

1 tsp (5 mL) pure vanilla extract

Variation

Chocolate Peanut Butter Pudding: Use 2 Tbsp (30 mL) peanut butter in place of the tahini and use 2 Tbsp (30 mL) cocoa powder in place of the vanilla.

Chunky Oil-Free Granola

Makes 2 lb/900 g granola (about 10 cups/2.5 L)

How can I express my undying love for granola? It's crunchy, it's sweet, it's nutritious. It's extremely filling without making you feel heavy. It's easy to make and it lasts for weeks. Kids can snack on it dry and it's a great camping breakfast. Granola is the best. I make it a little differently each time; here, I give you options for a few different combos—so think of this recipe as a template of sorts. I gravitate toward walnuts, pumpkin seeds, and tahini, but I do like to mix it up to keep things interesting and to ensure nutritional variation.

1. Preheat the oven to 325°F (160°C).

2. In a large bowl, combine the oats, chopped nuts, pumpkin or sunflower seeds, hemp seeds, cinnamon, and salt.

3. In a small bowl, stir or whisk together the maple syrup, tahini or peanut butter, and vanilla.

4. Pour the wet ingredients into the dry, and mix well until thoroughly combined.

5. Using your mixing utensil, spread the mixture onto a large baking sheet and pat down firmly and evenly.

6. Bake for 25 minutes, or until browning and starting to smell toasty.

7. Allow to cool fully before breaking up into chunks. Granola stored in an airtight container in the pantry keeps for several weeks.

4½ cups (1.125 L) rolled oats

1 cup (250 mL) chopped walnuts, pecans, and/or almonds

⅔ cup (160 mL) raw pumpkin and/or sunflower seeds

⅓ cup (80 mL) hemp seeds

1 tsp (5 mL) cinnamon

½ tsp (2 mL) salt

½ cup (125 mL) pure maple syrup

½ cup (125 mL) tahini or natural peanut butter

2 tsp (10 mL) pure vanilla extract

Blender Oat Pancakes

Serves 4

When the boys want a change from their usual oatmeal breakfast, we sometimes make these oat pancakes, which are essentially oatmeal in pancake form. My kids also like these as snacks or tucked into packed lunches. The flax seeds do double duty by acting as a binder and adding omega-3 fats. The batter comes together entirely in the blender and can be poured directly into the pan, keeping fuss and cleanup to a minimum.

1. Put the oats, flax seeds, milk, maple syrup (if using), baking powder, cinnamon, vanilla, and salt in a blender and blend on high until smooth. Set the batter aside for 5 to 10 minutes to allow the oats to hydrate and the mixture to thicken.

2. Meanwhile, heat a large pan over medium heat (see Tip).

3. Swirl a thin layer of oil into the pan and pour the batter into roughly 5-inch (13 cm) circles. You should be able to pour two or three circles, depending on the size of your pan.

4. Cook until bubbles start to form in the top of the pancakes and they turn matte, about 3 minutes. The undersides should be browning.

5. Flip and brown on the other side, 1 or 2 more minutes. Set on a wire rack or serve immediately. Repeat with the remaining batter.

6. Refrigerate any leftover pancakes in an airtight container for 2 to 3 days. Reheat by popping into the toaster.

1½ cups (375 mL) oats

2 Tbsp (30 mL) flax seeds

2 cups (500 mL) soy milk or other plant-based milk

3 Tbsp (45 mL) pure maple syrup (optional)

1½ tsp (7 mL) baking powder

1 tsp (5 mL) cinnamon

1 tsp (5 mL) pure vanilla extract

¼ tsp (1 mL) salt

Oil, for the pan

Tip

When making pancakes or crepes, it may take some experimenting to find which temperature works best on your particular stove. Medium heat is a good place to start. You want the pancakes to cook through while also forming a nice brown exterior. Too little heat, and the pancakes won't brown before cooking through. Too much heat, and the pancakes will brown before the batter is cooked through. Play around until you find the sweet spot on your stove. Once you've found it, I think you'll find that pancakes are very easy to make.

Hands-Off Creamy Oatmeal

Serves 2 to 3

Oats are a versatile and convenient breakfast food. Instead of boiling the oats in water only, I use half plant-based milk, which adds creaminess and nutrition. And I turn off the heat to let the oats steam, which frees me from stirring duty so I can do other morning things, like pack lunches and participate in dance parties.

1. Combine the oats, milk, and water in a medium saucepan with a lid.

2. Set over medium or medium-high heat and, stirring often, bring the mixture to a simmer. Put the lid on and remove from heat. Allow to sit, covered and undisturbed, for at least 10 minutes.

3. When the time is up, give the oatmeal a vigorous stir to help the starches release and thicken.

4. Stir in the hemp seeds, if using, and the maple syrup.

1 cup (250 mL) rolled oats

1 cup (250 mL) plant-based milk, plus more for serving

1 cup (250 mL) water

1½ Tbsp (22 mL) hemp seeds (optional)

2 Tbsp (30 mL) pure maple syrup, or to taste

Variations

Strawberries and Cream: Stir in a handful of fresh or frozen strawberries along with the oats, milk, and water in step 1. After serving, top with sliced fresh strawberries and a splash of plant-based milk or cream.

Apple Cinnamon: Core and finely chop 1 apple. Add to the pot of oats, milk, and water in step 1, along with 1 tsp (5 mL) cinnamon.

Cinnamon Raisin: Add a handful of raisins and 1 tsp (5 mL) cinnamon to the pot of oats, milk, and water in step 1.

Stewed Plum with Cardamom: Pit and chop 3 to 4 fresh plums and put in the empty pot, along with 2 to 3 crushed cardamom pods or ¼ tsp (1 mL) ground cardamom, and 1 Tbsp (15 mL) water. Cook the plums until they start to break down. Add the oats, milk, and water, and proceed with the recipe. Remove any cardamom pods before serving.

Mixed Berry and Banana: Mash 1 banana in the empty pot, and then add a handful of frozen mixed berries. Add the oats, milk, and water and proceed with the recipe.

Tip

We like to sometimes add chia seeds, too. I add 1 Tbsp (15 mL) chia seeds along with the oats in step 1, and an additional 3 Tbsp (45 mL) water.

Cinnamon-Flax French Toast

Serves 3 to 4

French toast has always felt a bit magical to me, because the *best* bread for it is old, stale, and dry—it's a sponge for the aromatic batter. While all cooking is alchemy, it feels particularly satisfying to transform something nearly inedible into a delicious meal. We make French toast sometimes for a more special weekday breakfast that doesn't require much time or effort. Make the batter the night before and refrigerate in a jar to simplify the morning.

1. In a wide, flat bowl that allows for bread dipping, whisk together the flax seed, chickpea flour, kala namak, and cinnamon. Slowly whisk in the milk. Set aside for a minute to allow the flax to thicken.

2. Preheat a wide skillet over medium heat. Dip both sides of a slice of bread in the batter, allowing the excess to drip off. Swirl a thin layer of oil in the pan and fry the battered bread until brown and crisp, about 3 minutes. Flip and brown the other side, then remove to a wire rack or serve immediately with a drizzle of maple syrup. Repeat with the remaining slices of bread.

2 Tbsp (30 mL) ground flax seed (see Tip)

2 Tbsp (30 mL) chickpea flour

¼ tsp (1 mL) kala namak (see Tip on page 63) or regular salt

¾ tsp (3 mL) cinnamon

⅔ cup (160 mL) plant-based milk

6 slices stale sandwich bread

Oil, for the pan

Pure maple syrup, for serving

Tip

We buy whole flax seeds and use our coffee grinder to grind them up as we need them. Alternatively, either buy flax seeds pre-ground (but please store them in the fridge or freezer—after being ground, the oil in them degrades more quickly) or simply start with whole flax seeds and make this batter in a blender.

Peanut Butter Banana Waffles with Berry Chia Sauce (page 51)

Tip

Do you need to oil your waffle maker?
I do, because I like the crispy exterior that
results from just a small amount of oil, and
it ensures the waffles are easy to remove.
If you'd like to keep the recipe oil-free and
you're using a non-stick waffle maker, you
should be able to get away with using no oil.
If the waffle does stick, use a rubber spatula
to gently lift the waffle off the hot element.

Gluten-Free Waffles, Four Ways

I have a small city kitchen, so I resist acquiring new appliances. For the longest time I didn't have a waffle maker, but I eventually caved and bought one because my kids like waffles, and I didn't want to be buying the over-packaged frozen kinds that cost too much and taste like sweetened corrugated cardboard. Arden and I are now the proud parents of an 8-inch (20 cm) round Belgian waffle maker, which is what these recipes were created on. It has turned out to be a fantastic purchase. Crisp on the outside and fluffy on the inside, fresh waffles have a dreamy texture. They're easy to make. They store well for future quick breakfasts. And you can use wholesome flours, transforming them into something even pickier eaters will go for. I'm a convert. I now wholeheartedly believe that any household with kids should consider adding a waffle maker to the family.

Oat Waffles

Makes five 8-inch (20 cm) waffles

These delicious waffles are so easy to make, nutritious, and filling. They're probably my kids' all-around favourite. They feel simple enough to pull off on weekdays, and we often do.

1. Put all the ingredients in a blender and blend on high until smooth.

2. Set the batter aside for 5 to 10 minutes to allow the oats to hydrate and the mixture to thicken.

3. Preheat the waffle maker to medium-high. Oil the waffle maker (see Tip), pour in a fifth of the batter (eyeball it!), and close the lid. Cook until the steam has subsided and the waffle is golden brown, about 6 minutes. Remove to a wire rack to keep crisp, or serve immediately. Repeat with the remaining batter.

4. Refrigerate any leftover waffles in an airtight container for 2 to 3 days and reheat by popping into the toaster. Waffles can also be frozen for up to 3 months.

2 cups (500 mL) rolled oats

2½ cups (625 mL) plant-based milk

3 Tbsp (45 mL) pure maple syrup (optional)

2 Tbsp (30 mL) chia seeds

1½ tsp (7 mL) baking powder

1 tsp (5 mL) cinnamon

Variations

With fruit: To any of the sweet waffles—that's the first three—add blueberries, chopped strawberries, or your other favourite fruit to the batter just before pouring into the waffle maker.

Chocolate chip: Fold ¼ to ⅓ cup (60 to 80 mL) dairy-free dark chocolate chips into the batter of any of the sweet waffles just before pouring into the waffle maker. (This is how my youngest son likes his best.)

recipe continues

Almond Waffles

Makes three 8-inch (20 cm) waffles

These waffles are light and satisfyingly chewy, and the natural fat in the almond flour helps create an incredibly crisp exterior. They're not only gluten-free but grain-free as well.

1. Preheat the waffle maker to medium-high.

2. In a large bowl, whisk together the almond flour, tapioca flour, and baking powder. Make a well in the dry ingredients and pour in the milk and maple syrup. Stir until a smooth batter forms— don't worry about overmixing, as there is no gluten here to become tough.

3. Oil the waffle maker (see Tip), scoop ½ heaping cup (150 mL) batter into the centre of the waffle maker, and close the lid. Cook until the steam has subsided and the waffle is golden brown, about 5 minutes. Remove to a wire rack to keep crisp, or serve immediately. Repeat with the remaining batter.

4. These waffles are best fresh, though you can refrigerate any leftover waffles in an airtight container for 2 to 3 days and reheat by popping into the toaster.

1½ cups (375 mL) almond flour

½ cup (125 mL) tapioca flour

1½ tsp (7 mL) baking powder

¾ cup (185 mL) plant-based milk

2 Tbsp (30 mL) pure maple syrup

Peanut Butter Banana Waffles

Makes five 8-inch (20 cm) waffles

I love to make these for my kids because they're packed with good ingredients that keep them well fuelled, and they're naturally sweetened from the ripe banana. To make them nut-free, use tahini in place of peanut butter.

1. Put all the ingredients in a blender and blend on high until smooth.

2. Set the batter aside for 5 to 10 minutes to allow the oats to hydrate and the mixture to thicken.

3. Preheat the waffle maker to medium-high. Oil the waffle maker (see Tip), pour in a fifth of the batter (eyeball it!), and close the lid. Cook until the steam has subsided and the waffle is golden brown, about 5 minutes. Remove to a wire rack to keep crisp, or serve immediately. Repeat with the remaining batter.

4. Refrigerate any leftover waffles in an airtight container for 2 to 3 days and reheat by popping into the toaster. Waffles can also be frozen for up to 3 months.

2 ripe bananas

1½ cups (375 mL) rolled oats

½ cup (125 mL) natural peanut butter (or tahini)

1¾ cups (435 mL) plant-based milk

2 Tbsp (30 mL) chia seeds

1½ tsp (7 mL) baking powder

2 tsp (10 mL) pure vanilla extract

Savoury Chickpea Waffles

Makes four 8-inch (20 cm) waffles

Why yes, I do use chickpea flour for everything. These light and crispy waffles make a yummy brunch sandwich when slathered with your fave fixings, such as vegan mayo, smoked tofu, fresh tomato, and crisp lettuce. I also love an Indian-influenced combination of unsweetened coconut yogurt, thinly sliced red onion, chopped tomato, and cilantro. I've even been known to top these with maple syrup and serve them to pickier eaters to get those legumes in.

1. In a large bowl, whisk together all the ingredients, adding the water slowly at first to prevent clumping.

2. Set the batter aside for at least 10 minutes to allow the flour to hydrate.

3. Preheat the waffle maker to medium-high. Oil the waffle maker (see Tip), pour in a quarter of the batter, and close the lid. Cook until the steam has subsided and the waffle is golden brown, about 6 minutes. Remove to a wire rack to keep crisp, or serve immediately. Repeat with the remaining batter.

4. These waffles are best fresh, though leftovers can be refrigerated in an airtight container for 2 to 3 days. Reheat by popping into the toaster.

2 cups (500 mL) chickpea flour

1½ cups (375 mL) water

1½ tsp (7 mL) baking powder

½ tsp (2 mL) salt

1 Tbsp (15 mL) avocado oil

Fried No-Egg Sandwich

Makes 1 big sandwich

One day I was browsing a food website, as one does, and noticed a fried-egg sandwich that had me reminiscing about the gooey-crispy fried-egg sandwiches of my youth. Upon experimenting, I was happy to learn that this effect is easy enough to recreate with chickpea flour crepes.

There are two main types of chickpeas that you'll commonly find ground into flour: desi chickpeas and kabuli chickpeas (also known as garbanzo beans). I find that desi chickpea flour, which may be labelled as besan or gram flour and is popular in Indian cuisine, is a little finer of the two, and it easily produces a thin, soft crepe that holds together without cracking or sticking. It's my preferred choice for this recipe. If you're shopping in North America and the chickpea flour you're using doesn't specify what type it is, assume it's made from kabuli chickpeas. Kabuli chickpea flour can work too—simply add an additional 2 to 3 Tbsp (30 to 45 mL) water and you'll get a tasty crepe (I do this myself when it's all I have). But if you can, check Indian grocers or the international food aisle at your supermarket for besan. In Vancouver, I can find big bags of it for super cheap at Real Canadian Superstore and No Frills.

1. In a small bowl, whisk together the besan, water, and kala namak. Set batter aside for 10 minutes to allow the flour to hydrate.

2. Preheat a large pan over medium heat. Swirl in a thin layer of oil and add the batter, forming an even-ish circle (you may need to shake or swirl the pan).

3. Cook the crepe for 3 to 4 minutes, until the top is opaque—you'll be able to smell it getting toasty, and a peek at the bottom will reveal a nice brown underside. There's no need to flip the crepe, as it will be cooked through at this point and you want it to stay soft and pliable.

4. To make it easier to build the sandwich, use your spatula to fold in the edges of the crepe to roughly the size and shape of your bread.

5. Place the crepe on 1 slice of bread and continue to build your sandwich with your toppings of choice. Top with the remaining slice of bread.

⅓ cup (80 mL) besan (Indian chickpea flour)

⅓ cup (80 mL) + 1 Tbsp (15 mL) water (see Tips)

¼ tsp (1 mL) kala namak or regular salt (see Tips)

Oil, for the pan

2 slices bread of your choice, toasted if you'd like

Other sandwich toppings: vegan butter, vegan mayo, mustard, ketchup, vegan cheese, lettuce, arugula, tomato slices

Tips

If you're using kabuli chickpea flour rather than besan, add an additional 2 to 3 Tbsp (30 to 45 mL) water in step 1 to achieve a thin enough batter for this crepe. The batter should have the consistency of milk (more or less).

Kala namak is a salt seasoning that is traditionally used in South Asian cuisine. It has a complex flavour and pungent aroma, the most pronounced of which is sulphur—the same compound that gives cooked eggs their characteristic taste. Sometimes called black salt, kala namak is actually pink or purple when ground. You should be able to find it at Indian grocers, spice stores, or online.

Simple Scrambled Tofu

Serves 2 to 4

This is your super basic scrambled eggs swap: it's equally fast, easy, and delicious. We make it often on weekends and for big family brunches. A medium-firm tofu makes for a good scramble consistency, because it can be crumbled into soft curds that are reminiscent of scrambled eggs. Source kala namak (see Tip on page 63) if you like a really eggy flavour, which comes from the salt's sulphurous aroma compounds. Otherwise, regular salt will do.

1. Heat a skillet over medium heat. When hot, add the oil and turmeric. The turmeric will bubble slightly in the hot oil and start to toast. Stir it around a little until it has darkened a few shades, about 15 seconds.

2. Use your hands to crumble the tofu into the pan. Add the nutritional yeast, onion powder, and kala namak, and cook until warmed through, 1 or 2 minutes.

3. Refrigerate any leftovers in an airtight container for up to 4 to 5 days.

1 tsp (5 mL) oil

¼ tsp (1 mL) turmeric

1 (12 oz/350 g) block medium-firm tofu

1 Tbsp (15 mL) nutritional yeast

½ tsp (2 mL) onion powder

½ tsp (2 mL) kala namak or regular salt

Make it a meal

For breakfast: Serve scrambled tofu with toast and fruit.

On weekends: We like our scrambled tofu with roasted potatoes and vegan sausage.

Make brunch tacos: Warm corn tortillas in a separate pan, then spoon on some scrambled tofu, and add a few crisp, tangy, and/or creamy toppings like sliced avocado, Quick-Pickled Cabbage or Onion (page 152), Super Speedy Salsa (page 155), shredded lettuce, Cilantro-Lime Cream (page 155), thinly sliced radish, fresh cilantro or parsley, chopped green onion, and all the hot sauce.

Brunch Hash

Serves 4

On weekends when we have leftover roasted potatoes or sweet potatoes (which is often), we love to use them to make a big skillet of brunch hash. Roasted regular potatoes in particular don't reheat well, and this is the best way I've found to give them a delicious second life. Creating a spice blend and whisking it with water to make a sauce helps get flavour into all the nooks and crannies of the tofu while keeping things moist. And the toasted fennel seeds add a sausagey taste and aroma. This is a complete meal on its own, but sometimes we like to also fold it into warm corn tortillas, maybe with a little avocado and green onion, and definitely with plenty of hot sauce for me.

1. In a small bowl, whisk together the nutritional yeast, garlic powder, salt, turmeric, and a few grinds of pepper. Pour in the water and whisk to form a sauce.

2. Heat a wide skillet over medium heat. Add the oil and fennel seeds. Toast the fennel seeds just until they start to brown.

3. Add the onion and sauté for a few minutes until it starts to sweat. It doesn't need to be fully soft or translucent—some crisp texture is good.

4. Crumble in the tofu and increase the heat to medium-high. After a few minutes, when the tofu is cooked through and starting to brown a little, reduce the heat to medium, add the spice sauce, and stir to combine. The liquid should absorb quickly.

5. Add the potatoes just to warm through, 1 or 2 minutes. If they seem dry, add a splash of water.

6. Refrigerate any leftovers in an airtight container for up to 3 to 4 days.

2 Tbsp (30 mL) nutritional yeast

1 tsp (5 mL) garlic powder

¾ tsp (3 mL) salt

½ tsp (2 mL) turmeric

Freshly ground pepper

¼ cup (60 mL) water

2 to 3 tsp (10 to 15 mL) avocado oil

1 tsp (5 mL) fennel seeds

½ onion, diced

1 (12 oz/350 g) block extra-firm tofu

3 cups (750 mL) leftover roasted potatoes or sweet potatoes, cut into cubes if they aren't already (see Tip)

Tip

If you don't have leftover roasted potatoes, no problem! Make some by chopping about 1 lb (454 g) potatoes or sweet potatoes into bite-sized cubes, tossing with a little oil and salt, and spreading evenly on a baking sheet. Bake at 400°F (200°C) for 30 to 40 minutes, until brown and tender, flipping after 20 minutes.

Lunch

While dinner can be a time to slow our pace, cook a proper meal, and sit down with loved ones to savour it, lunch is often in the midst of a busy day, when we don't have the mental bandwidth to devote much time or attention to our food. I try to get everyone eating more or less the same thing for dinner, which in practice means cooking common denominator meals that all family members will be content with. But at lunch time, we all follow our personal preferences a bit more.

If we're eating out of the house, lunch needs to be portable, and often something that can be enjoyed at room temperature. So you'll find in this chapter sections on how to make a good (filling!) salad and how to pack a kid's lunchbox. I've also included recipes for my go-to hearty salads, sandwiches, and nori rolls, all of which are portable and still delicious hours after being packed.

As you've likely picked up on by now, I log most of my cooking hours at dinnertime from Monday to Thursday. My strategy is to cook large quantities so that the fridge is stocked with intentional leftovers, which make for quick and easy lunches. Pastas and stir-fries can be heated as is. Soups and stews make for excellent leftovers, because the flavours deepen with time, and they transport well in thermoses. When I make grains, starches, beans, and veggies for bowls, I scale up as if I'm feeding a gymnastics team.

My kids like to pack sandwiches for school lunches. My eldest son, Harlan, loves Chickpea Salad Sandwiches (page 88), while my younger son, Alister—who inherited his dad's sweet tooth—prefers a Grilled Peanut Butter and Banana Sandwich (page 90) with its melty dark chocolate chips. For myself, I love to make a big salad for lunches at home or on the go; my preferences change slightly with the seasons, as you'll see in my Herby Summer Salad with Quinoa and Dates (page 78) and Winter Kale Salad with Sweet Potato and White Bean Purée (page 79). When I need a midday noodle fix in under 10 minutes, I also love to make my quick Sesame Soba Noodles with Kale and Edamame—extra hot sauce, please.

How to Make a Good Salad

A good salad can be flavourful and hearty, filling you up but not weighing you down. My favourite salads have a base of dark green leafy veggies, crisp and juicy veggies, legumes and grains or starches in some form, satiating quality fats, and a delicious dressing. Here's how I do it.

Start with a base of greens

When is it a salad and when is it a bowl? I don't think there's any clear consensus delineating the two, but here's how I think of it: A salad starts with a base of greens and may include grains or starches. A bowl starts with a base of grains or starches and may include greens.

Lettuce is an obvious green to include, and in supermarkets these days there are all kinds of varieties. Good ol' leaf lettuce is one of my favourites. Lettuce is also easy to grow if you have a small patch of sun—it only needs a shallow amount of soil and it grows quickly. Baby greens of all kinds are tender enough to eat raw, from chard to fava tips to sorrel. Spinach, arugula, and kale are all great, too, either on their own or combined with lettuce or other greens. I find that heartier greens are best when finely chopped—big pieces can be hard to chew.

Pile on the veggies

Beyond greens, other veggies are an opportunity to add colour and texture: red or green cabbage, colourful peppers, white or red onions, green onions, snap peas, carrots, tomatoes, avocado, and cucumber are my go-tos. Soft or juicy ingredients, like avocados and cut tomatoes (as opposed to uncut cherry tomatoes), will meld into the dressing, distributing their delicious flavour throughout.

How you cut or prepare the vegetables makes a difference, too. My preference is for smaller cuts, which ensures a variety of veggies in each bite. Hard vegetables, like cabbage and carrot, are best shredded or cut finely instead of cut into chunks, in my opinion.

I love adding flavourful roasted vegetables to salads as well. Consider roasting a big tray of veggies and keeping them in the fridge for future quick salads. Some veggies that are especially good roasted are broccoli and cauliflower, squash (all types), eggplant, and root veggies like beets, turnips, parsnips, sunchokes, carrots, and sweet potatoes.

Add a source of concentrated protein

I don't consider a salad complete until it includes a source of concentrated protein, ideally a legume in some form. These are some of my favourites:

- Straight-up rinsed legumes, like chickpeas, cannellini (white kidney) beans, French lentils, and black beans. They don't need any special treatment because they'll be flavoured by the dressing. Rinsed canned legumes work well here if you don't have any cooked from dried.

- Legumes tossed in herbs and spices, like paprika, garlic powder, or oregano, and pan-fried until crisped and fragrant. Generally I don't bother with the effort of seasoning legumes unless I already have them as leftovers from Tuesday bowls (see my Lemon-Garlic Cannellini Beans on page 138 and my Five-Minute Paprika-Spiked Chickpeas and Greens on page 140 for examples).
- Tofu or tempeh, pan-fried with a little soy sauce.
- Oil-Free Hummus (page 214) or White Bean Purée (page 215), which not only add protein and fat but also contribute to the dressing.
- Nuts and seeds. I consider these complementary to my legume, not a replacement, but I'm not the boss of you. Toast them for extra deliciousness.
- Quinoa and amaranth, cooled slightly or straight from the fridge. These so-called pseudo-cereal grains are higher in protein than cereal grains, like rice.

Include fats

A low-fat salad is a fast track to dissatisfaction and hunger. We need fats not only to make us feel satiated, but to help us absorb important fat-soluble vitamins A, D, E, and K.

- Dressings are an obvious way to incorporate healthy fats. I usually use dressings based on extra virgin olive oil or tahini (see the recipes at the end of this section). Other nut and seed butters, like almond butter, also make great dressing bases, as does unsweetened coconut yogurt.
- Add an avocado, either sliced on top or chopped up and distributed throughout, where it melds into the salad.
- All manner of nuts and seeds are delicious in salads. I like to chop most nuts, to help distribute them throughout the salad and make them easier to spear with my fork. Try sunflower seeds, pine nuts, and chopped macadamia nuts.
- Toasting nuts and seeds makes them especially flavourful; they can also be purchased toasted. My favourites are toasted pumpkin seeds, toasted sesame seeds, chopped toasted almonds, and chopped toasted walnuts.
- I almost always sprinkle some hemp seeds on salads, too. They're so nutritious, and being soft and mild, they sort of disappear into the salad.

Don't forget about starches and grains

Starches and grains might just be the real secret of a salad that can keep you full until dinner.

- Soft, caramel-y roasted sweet potatoes are one of my favourite salad ingredients. I either roast them whole and pile my salad on top, or cut them into cubes so I can distribute them throughout.
- Although regular potatoes don't keep well once roasted, boiled potatoes can make a fantastic salad add-in—just ask the millions of people who enjoy potato salad every summer. Boiled potatoes soak up dressing and become *so* delicious.
- Cooled quinoa, amaranth, and millet are fantastic and filling whole food options.

- Make it a noodle salad by including soba or thin rice noodles. If you need inspiration, see my Sesame Soba Noodles with Kale and Edamame (page 80)—one of my favourite lunches.
- Cooled short pasta pairs so well with a salad dressing, beans, and some crisp veggies. Even people who are still learning to love salads have probably enjoyed a southwest-style pasta salad, perhaps with black beans and corn.

Consider a pop of something sweet

Salads are generally tossed in a vinegary or citrusy dressing. I find the sourness can sometimes grow tiresome without a contrasting sweet ingredient to keep things balanced. Once again, my favourite sweet potatoes come to the rescue here. Other delicious options include chopped dates, raisins, shredded or roasted carrots or beets (they're especially sweet when roasted), and corn.

Throw in some fresh herbs

I'm a big fan of herbs in salads. And not just a cute little garnish either, but handfuls of them. Why not? They are, by design, intensely flavourful. Try cilantro, parsley, mint, dill, chives, basil, and anything else you can grow or find. Use them alone to allow their unique flavour to come through, or in combination to keep things interesting. See my Herby Summer Salad with Quinoa and Dates (page 78) for an example.

Tie it together with a dressing

Dressing is essential—we agree on that, right? I don't think there's anything wrong with store-bought dressing, especially if having a bottle of dressing in the fridge is what gets you eating salad. My only unsolicited mom advice is to check the ingredient labels and select one with quality oils (such as cold- or expeller-pressed) and no preservatives.

I don't generally bother with premade dressings, though, because it's so easy to just whisk together some oil and vinegar or citrus using ingredients I already have in my kitchen. These homemade dressings taste good, include high-quality ingredients and less oil than most store-bought versions, and don't clutter up my fridge with extra bottles.

Following are a few of my favourite simple, whisk-able dressings. They all make around ¼ cup (60 mL) of dressing, but you can double the recipe if you're making more than two servings. Always taste and adjust the dressing to your taste preferences for salty, creamy, sweet, and sour. Remember that a dressing's flavour will be more concentrated when tasted directly than when tossed with the salad.

Everyday Vinaigrette

Whisk together 1½ Tbsp (22 mL) extra virgin olive oil, 1 Tbsp (15 mL) red wine vinegar, 2 tsp (10 mL) Dijon mustard, 1 to 2 tsp (5 to 10 mL) pure maple syrup, and a pinch of salt. Alternatively, substitute any other vinegar you have for the red wine vinegar: apple cider, rice, and balsamic work nicely.

Lemon-Garlic Vinaigrette

Whisk together 2 Tbsp (30 mL) extra virgin olive oil, 1 Tbsp (15 mL) freshly squeezed lemon juice, 1 tsp (5 mL) Dijon mustard, 1 minced garlic clove, and a pinch of salt. Optionally add the zest of the lemon for added lemon flavour without additional sourness. If it's too sour, add 1 to 2 tsp (5 to 10 mL) pure maple syrup to balance it out.

Creamy Tahini Caesar Dressing

Whisk together 1½ Tbsp (22 mL) tahini, 1 Tbsp (15 mL) freshly squeezed lemon juice, 1 Tbsp (15 mL) water, ½ Tbsp (7 mL) minced capers, 1 tsp (5 mL) caper brine, and 1 minced garlic clove. Add more water if you find the dressing is too thick (tahini can vary in consistency).

Tip

To save on dishes, whisk your dressing together in the salad bowl before adding the veggies.

Creamy Tahini Caesar Dressing

Herby Summer Salad
with Quinoa and Dates

Serves 2

Bringing fresh herbs to centre stage rather than using them strictly as a garnish is an easy way to add lots of flavour. When my garden is bursting with herbs and greens, I love to make a pot of quinoa and some tangy dressing to turn them into a refreshing summer lunch.

1. Put the quinoa and ¾ cup (185 mL) water in a small saucepan. Simmer, covered, for 10 minutes. Without removing the lid, remove from the heat and allow to steam for 5 minutes. Then transfer the quinoa to a wide bowl to cool until it's no longer steaming so it doesn't wilt your greens.

2. To the cooled quinoa, add the lettuce, arugula, herbs, tomatoes, and dates. Drizzle on the vinaigrette until your desired sauciness level is reached. If you don't need the entire batch of dressing, store any extra in a jar on the counter for your next salad.

½ cup (125 mL) uncooked quinoa

3 to 4 gently packed cups (750 mL to 1 L) chopped lettuce

1 to 2 gently packed cups (250 to 500 mL) chopped arugula

A big handful each of at least two kinds of fresh herbs (cilantro, basil, mint, dill, chives), coarsely chopped

¾ cup (185 mL) chopped tomatoes

½ cup (125 mL) pitted and chopped dates

Double batch Everyday Vinaigrette (page 76)

Variation

With chickpeas: Bulk up this salad by adding 1 cup (250 mL) rinsed chickpeas.

Winter Kale Salad with Sweet Potato and White Bean Purée

Serves 2

With the roasted sweet potato, this salad feels warm and hearty enough even for cool winter days. Although I'm providing instructions for all the components, in reality I would never do all this work at once for just one meal. Rather, as I'm cooking throughout the week, I make extras: roasted sweet potatoes reheat well and they make a great base for so many meals; toasted pumpkin seeds keep for weeks on the counter and add crunch and flavour to bowls, tacos, and salads; and white bean purée is perfect for snacks and sandwiches, too. Fill your baking sheet with sweet potatoes and your skillet with pumpkin seeds, if you'd like, as I do. I'm always grateful at lunch time when I have at least one or two things already prepared.

1. Preheat the oven to 400°F (200°C).

2. Scrub the sweet potato and cut in half lengthwise. Lightly rub all over with oil and place cut side down on a baking sheet. Sprinkle with salt. Roast for 30 to 35 minutes, or until a knife goes through the largest part of the potato with no resistance.

3. Heat a wide skillet over medium heat. Place the pumpkin seeds in the skillet, turning them often until they are deeply golden, 3 to 5 minutes.

4. Put the kale in a large bowl along with the avocado, vinegar, and ¼ tsp (1 mL) salt. Use a clean hand to massage the ingredients together. This will help coat the kale and tenderize it.

5. Add the cabbage and pumpkin seeds to the kale mixture and toss to mix.

6. Place a roasted sweet potato half, cut side up, on each of two plates. Divide the salad between the plates. Top with a large scoop of white bean purée.

1 medium sweet potato

Oil, for roasting

¼ tsp (1 mL) salt, plus more for roasting

⅓ cup (80 mL) raw pumpkin seeds

6 to 7 kale leaves, destemmed and thinly sliced

½ avocado, pitted, peeled, and cubed

4 tsp (20 mL) red wine vinegar

1 cup (250 mL) shredded red cabbage

⅔ cup (160 mL) White Bean Purée (page 215)

Sesame Soba Noodles with Kale and Edamame

Serves 2 to 3

Soba noodles are quick to cook and they work well at room temperature, making them a natural choice for a quick or make-ahead lunch. You could even whip up this dish before leaving the house, as it comes together in one pot in under 10 minutes. Although it includes only a few ingredients, it is very flavourful—soy sauce and sesame oil bring so much to the table.

1. Boil the noodles and edamame together until both are tender, 3 to 4 minutes (double check your packages to make sure this is the correct cooking time, as there may be some variation). Drain and rinse under warm water to prevent clumping.

2. Toss the cooked noodles and edamame with soy sauce, sesame oil, hot sauce (if using), and kale. Taste and adjust the flavours.

3. Refrigerate any leftovers for up to 2 to 3 days.

6 oz (180 g) soba noodles

1 cup (250 mL) frozen shelled edamame

¼ cup (60 mL) soy sauce

1½ Tbsp (22 mL) sesame oil

1 tsp (5 mL) Sriracha or other chili-garlic hot sauce (optional)

2 cups (500 mL) finely chopped kale

Parsley Salad with Cannellini Beans and Millet

Serves 4

This fresh, simple dish is inspired by tabbouleh, the delicious and traditionally vegetarian Middle Eastern salad that features parsley as the main green. I use millet instead of the traditional bulgur or cracked wheat; it has a similar size and texture. I also add creamy cannellini beans to make it a complete meal. If you invite me to an adults-only potluck on a hot day, there's a decent chance this is what I'll bring.

1. Put the millet, 1 cup (250 mL) water, and a pinch of salt into a large saucepan. Bring to a boil and simmer, covered, for 15 minutes. Remove from the heat and let stand, covered, for 10 minutes to steam. Remove the lid and fluff with a fork. Set aside to cool a bit while you prepare the rest of the salad.

2. Meanwhile, in a large bowl, whisk together the lemon zest and juice, olive oil, garlic, and maple syrup. Season with salt and pepper.

3. Add the beans and millet to the dressing and toss to coat. Stir in the bell pepper, parsley, and tomato. If you can, let sit for 15 minutes to allow the flavours to absorb and meld. Taste and adjust the seasonings as needed.

4. Refrigerate any leftovers in an airtight container for up to 2 to 3 days.

½ cup (125 mL) uncooked millet

Zest and juice of 2 lemons

3 Tbsp (45 mL) extra virgin olive oil

3 cloves garlic, minced

1 to 2 tsp (5 to 10 mL) pure maple syrup, to taste

Salt and pepper

2 cups (500 mL) cooked cannellini (white kidney) beans, rinsed

1 orange or yellow bell pepper, diced

1 bunch curly or flat-leaf parsley, finely chopped (about 2 cups/ 500 mL)

1 cup (250 mL) diced tomatoes

Basic Baked Tofu

Makes enough for 4 sandwiches

When baked, tofu takes on chewy texture that's so satisfying in sandwiches. It's convenient to prepare a double batch to have on hand in the fridge throughout the week for packed lunches. With just a quick dip in soy sauce, these simple baked tofu slabs are versatile enough to use for many different flavour profiles. A couple of my favourite baked tofu sandwiches follow this recipe, but please do experiment!

1. Preheat the oven to 400°F (200°C), using the convection setting if you have it. Brush a baking sheet lightly with oil.

2. Slice the tofu into ⅓-inch (1 cm) thick slabs. (The tofu will shrink a bit in the oven.) Fold the tofu slabs into a clean tea towel and blot dry.

3. Pour the soy sauce into a small, flat-bottomed bowl. Dip both sides of the tofu in the soy sauce, shake off the excess, and place on the prepared baking sheet.

4. Bake for 20 minutes, flip, and bake for 10 more minutes. The tofu should look matte and richly brown.

5. Refrigerate in an airtight container for 4 to 5 days; baked tofu is great cold from the fridge.

1 (12 oz/350 g) block extra-firm tofu

1 Tbsp (15 mL) soy sauce

Cheater Bánh Mì

Serves 1

When the French colonized Vietnam, they brought French ingredients—including baguettes and mayonnaise—with them. This gave rise to the bánh mì sandwich, a fusion of French and Vietnamese flavours. I used to love to treat myself to a tofu bánh mì at a Vietnamese café, but since having kids, it feels easier to whip up a home-style version in my own kitchen. I love that I can use whole grain bread and organic veggies, and make extras for later (double or triple the recipe, if you'd like). Traditionally, bánh mì contains pickled carrot and daikon, but to make this speedier I simply toss grated carrot in a little rice vinegar.

1. In a small bowl, toss the carrot with the vinegar.
2. Slice the baguette in half lengthwise. Spread the mayo on both cut sides of the baguette. Layer on the tofu, cucumber, dressed carrot, and cilantro sprigs.

Tip

Although it's traditional to make bánh mì sandwiches using baguette, most of the time we don't have these in our kitchen, and you may not either. Regular sandwich bread works beautifully as well.

2 to 3 Tbsp (30 to 45 mL) grated carrot

½ tsp (2 mL) rice vinegar or other mild vinegar, like white or apple cider

1 (6-inch/16 cm) baguette, fresh or lightly toasted (see Tip)

1 Tbsp (15 mL) vegan mayo

2 to 3 pieces Basic Baked Tofu

2 to 3 Tbsp (30 to 45 mL) thinly sliced cucumber

5 or 6 cilantro sprigs, tough stems removed

Tofu, Lettuce, and Tomato

Serves 1

This is your classic lunch sandwich that's as good as it is simple. Switch up the veggies and condiments based on what you have and what you like.

1. Spread mayo or avocado on one side of each slice of toast. Add the mustard to one of the slices and top with the tofu, tomato, salt, pepper, and lettuce. Top with the other slice of toast.

Vegan mayo or avocado

2 slices sandwich bread, toasted

Dijon mustard

2 to 3 pieces Basic Baked Tofu (page 85)

1 vine-ripened tomato, sliced

Salt and pepper

Crisp lettuce, such as Romaine or butterhead

Chickpea Salad Sandwiches

Serves 3 to 4

I really liked tuna salad sandwiches as a kid, but since making them with mashed chickpeas in place of tuna, I've realized that it's really the flavourful additions—pickles, celery, mustard, mayo—that make them taste so good. Hearty mashed chickpeas have a great texture here; you won't miss the tuna. I love how quick and easy chickpea salad is to make, even last minute when I need a packed or picnic lunch in a hurry. In addition to being great on sandwiches, try chickpea salad with crackers for scooping, for a less-messy on-the-go snack for little people.

1. Put the chickpeas in a wide-bottomed bowl and, using a fork or potato masher, mash them until no whole chickpeas remain. There should still be some texture—you don't want purée.

2. Stir in the mayo, mustard, pickle, pickle brine, and celery. Taste and adjust to your preferences, seasoning with salt and pepper.

3. Serve on bread—open faced or between slices of bread—or with crackers.

4. Refrigerate leftover chickpea salad in an airtight container for 4 to 5 days.

1½ cups (375 mL) cooked chickpeas, drained and rinsed

2 Tbsp (30 mL) vegan mayo

2 tsp (10 mL) Dijon mustard

1 dill pickle, finely diced

2 tsp (10 mL) dill pickle brine

1 stalk celery, finely diced

Salt and pepper

Bread or crackers, for serving

Variation

Whole foods chickpea salad: In place of vegan mayo, try tahini or mashed avocado.

Grilled Peanut Butter and Banana Sandwich

Serves 1

Gooey grilled banana sandwiches with peanut butter and a hint of chocolate make an easy breakfast or lunch and are especially popular with kids. I've always loved the combination of peanut butter and chocolate, and now my kids are carrying on the noble tradition. And don't feel bad about the chocolate chips: dark chocolate is a source of iron. It's basically our duty to eat it.

1. Heat a pan over medium heat.

2. Spread a thin layer of vegan butter on one side of each slice of bread. This will be the outside of the sandwich.

3. Spread a layer of peanut butter on the other side of both slices of bread. On one slice, top the peanut butter with a layer of banana. Dot the chocolate chips between the bananas and press a few into the centre of the banana rounds. Top with the other slice of bread, peanut butter side down.

4. Toast the sandwich in the pan, flipping once, until golden on both sides. Transfer to a plate, slice diagonally, and serve.

Vegan butter

2 slices sandwich bread

1 to 2 Tbsp (15 to 30 mL) peanut butter

½ banana, sliced into ¼-inch (5 mm) rounds

1 Tbsp (15 mL) dairy-free dark chocolate chips

Variation

Make it peanut-free: Use almond butter, tahini, or another nut and seed butter in place of peanut butter.

How to Pack a Kid's Lunchbox

I'm packing lunches for my kids only a few days a week and their school day doesn't start until 10 a.m., so I must confess that I don't really have the right to grumble about packing school lunches. Still, I do it enough to understand why it is the bane of so many parents' existence. Feeding kids can be challenging at the best of times; on top of everything else, school lunches need to be portable, appetizing hours after they've been prepared, and put together in an already compressed morning. Depending on the school, they may need to be allergen-friendly, too. Here's how I approach packing lunches for my kids, who are still too young to pack their own:

Plan ahead

Ten minutes before we leave for school is a bad time to realize I need to roast a sweet potato or soak some chia pudding. The night before I pack school lunches, I try to turn my mind to any prepping ahead that will make my school-lunch packing a little easier in the morning. These tasks aren't typically very demanding, but they do require lead time, which means starting the night before is doing my future self a giant solid.

Don't be afraid of repetition

I brought the same school lunch almost every single day as a kid. Did I love it? Well, not really. Was I sufficiently nourished to learn and play? Absolutely. While I want my kids to explore new foods and eat a diverse diet, they can do this at dinner. Anyway, kids have their favourite foods, which they're happy enough to eat on repeat.

Get them to help

All kids can age-appropriately pitch in with packing their own lunches. At minimum, I get them to help brainstorm what lunch will be. In addition to being a practical way to determine what to pack, I like them to be aware that lunch doesn't magically pack itself, and to start to understand the responsibility and effort that go into feeding ourselves. Young kids can help pack their lunchbox, while older kids can start to actually make their own lunches.

Communicate

When my kids get home from school, I sometimes talk to them about what they ate and liked. If something didn't travel well, was too dry, or too messy, or too anything, I want to know about it for next time. I find that unless I ask them directly, it doesn't occur to them to bring it up.

Keep it simple

While I may enjoy balsamic roasted carrots drizzled with carrot-top pesto, my kids are happy with carrot sticks. School lunches are not the place for culinary statements. They like eating simple food and I like making simple food. Why complicate it?

What's in my kids' lunches?

I try to include a complex carbohydrate, a protein-rich food, a vegetable, and a fruit (you'll find specific ideas in the chart on the next page). One component might include several of these categories—such as nori rolls made with brown rice and tofu—but I still mentally run through them to make sure I'm putting together a balanced meal. I also usually include a little treat, like a square of dark chocolate, a cookie, or some non-terrible candies.

Sometimes my kids take sandwiches (including the ones you'll find the recipes for in this chapter), wraps, or bean quesadillas. If we have leftovers they like, I'll send those in a thermos—meals like pasta, soup, stew, or even oatmeal. Most often, they take a simple bento-style lunch that is a combination of the foods in the chart on the following page.

Balanced Lunchbox Mix and Match

COMPLEX CARBOHYDRATES

- Brown Rice Nori Rolls (page 96)
- Cereal
- Granola (page 52)
- Muffins and quick breads
- Oats: In the form of oatmeal (page 56), pancakes (page 55), cookies (pages 223 and 224), waffles (pages 59 and 60), energy bites
- Pasta
- Polenta
- Popcorn
- Rice cakes
- Rice or soba noodles
- Roasted sweet potato
- Tortillas
- Whole grain crackers
- Whole grain bread

VEGGIES

- Avocado
- Bell peppers (red, orange, yellow)
- Carrot sticks
- Celery
- Cherry tomatoes
- Corn
- Cucumber slices
- Green peas
- Green smoothies
- Pickles
- Snap peas

PROTEIN-RICH FOODS

- Almond Waffles (page 60)
- Baked beans
- Bean burger patties
- Chia pudding (page 51)
- Edamame
- Hummus (page 214)
- Nut and seed butters
- Refried beans
- Roasted chickpeas
- Soy milk
- Sunflower Carrot Nori Rolls (page 99)
- Tofu (page 142)
- Trail mix

FRUITS

- Apple
- Banana
- Blackberries
- Blueberries
- Berry Chia Sauce (page 51)
- Dried fruit (raisins, mango, apricots, dates, figs)
- Fruit smoothies
- Mango
- Nectarine
- Orange
- Peach
- Pear
- Persimmon
- Plum
- Raspberries
- Strawberries

Brown Rice Nori Rolls

Makes 4 large rolls (32 to 40 pieces)

This is my eldest son's absolute fave food. Often when we're having rice for dinner, I'll cook an extra 1 cup (250 mL) rice so I can make these rolls to tuck into packed lunches. You'll need a rolling mat for this, which you should be able to find at a kitchen or dollar store. It's not necessary to use sushi rice—I've found that brown jasmine rice, which seems to be softer than other varieties of brown rice, works very well. Whatever type of rice you're using, please use it when freshly cooked. Refrigerated rice isn't sticky enough (believe me, I've tried!)

1. Cook the rice according to the package directions, and allow it to cool until you can comfortably handle it.

2. In a large bowl, whisk together the maple syrup and vinegar. Add the rice and stir well to combine.

3. Place a nori sheet lengthwise on a rolling mat. Place a quarter of the seasoned rice on the half of the nori sheet closest to you. Using a small bowl of water or your tap, wet your fingers and gently pat the rice into an even layer.

4. Pile some filling ingredients in a row down the centre of the rice, and sprinkle ½ tsp (2 mL) sesame seeds over top.

5. Fold over the end closest to you so that the rice wraps around the fillings, tucking the roll in tightly. Continue to roll up the remaining nori and seal the long end by running some water along it using your finger. Set aside to soften while you make the remaining rolls.

6. When ready to serve, use your sharpest serrated knife to cut the rolls into bite-sized pieces, approximately 8 to 10 per roll. Serve the soy sauce alongside, for dipping. Refrigerate any extras for up to 3 days in an airtight container, uncut to prevent drying out.

1 cup (250 mL) uncooked brown jasmine rice

2 Tbsp (30 mL) pure maple syrup, coconut sugar, or other sugar

1½ Tbsp (22 mL) rice vinegar

4 dried nori sheets

Thinly sliced filling ingredients (see Tip)

2 tsp (10 mL) toasted sesame seeds, divided

Soy sauce for dipping, watered down a little for kids

Tip

Some of my kids' favourite fillings are sweet bell pepper, cucumber, avocado, roasted sweet potato, and tofu. I'm partial to cooked shiitake mushrooms, lettuce, and alfalfa sprouts. You can use one filling or several, but try not to overload it or the nori will be hard to roll, and even harder to eat. Aim for a maximum ¾-inch (2 cm) diameter of filling ingredients.

Sunflower Carrot Nori Rolls

Makes 4 large rolls (32 to 40 pieces)

These nori rolls contain only a few ingredients but have a complex flavour thanks to the miso and seaweed. The carrots add sweetness and, together with the sunflower seeds, create a satisfying body that makes a wonderful alternative to rice. These make a great addition to lunchboxes for kids and adults alike. I also serve them as an easy, delicious finger food when we have friends or family over.

1. To soften the sunflower seeds, put in a small bowl, pour boiling water over them, and then let sit for 30 minutes. Drain.

2. Put the sunflower seeds, carrots, and miso in a food processor. Pulse until an even pâté forms.

3. Place a nori sheet lengthwise on a rolling mat. Gently and evenly spread a quarter of the pâté on the half of the nori sheet closest to you.

4. Pile some filling ingredients in a row down the centre of the pâté.

5. Fold over the end closest to you so that the rice wraps around the fillings, tucking the roll in tightly. Continue to roll up the remaining nori and seal the long end by running some water along it using your finger. Set aside to soften while you make the remaining rolls.

6. When ready to serve, use your sharpest serrated knife to cut the rolls into bite-sized pieces, approximately 8 to 10 per roll. Serve the soy sauce alongside, for dipping. Refrigerate any extras for up to 3 days in an airtight container, uncut to prevent drying out.

1 cup (250 mL) raw sunflower seeds

2 medium carrots, scrubbed or peeled and chopped into chunks

2 Tbsp (30 mL) white miso

4 dried nori sheets

Thinly sliced filling ingredients (see Tip on page 96)

Soy sauce for dipping, watered down a little for kids

Pasta Monday

Since I started cooking by theme, I've come to really love having pasta on Mondays. Pasta dishes are typically on the easy side, making it an approachable way to get dinner on the table on that first post-weekend day. Maybe more than that, pasta is just one of those comfort meals that everyone seems to love. Even on the Monday-est of Mondays, I can always look forward to a cozy bowl of pasta with my favourite people.

When I was growing up, my favourite pasta sauce was of the rich and creamy variety. I loved fettuccine Alfredo, and macaroni and cheese—but these dairy-heavy foods gave me heartburn and left me feeling lethargic. These days, I still enjoy my creamy pastas, using whole plant foods instead. Not only do these plant-based versions align better with my values, they don't weigh me down. You might even say it's pasta that loves me back. One of my long-time go-to creamy pasta dishes, which has now become a family favourite, is the very easy Basic Cashew Cream Pasta (page 108). And I've made my veggie-based Mac and Cheesy with Broccoli (page 112) for countless kids and adults who've said they couldn't tell it was vegan.

Pesto pasta is another of those dishes that I've long loved; it must be one of the most delicious ways in the world to eat leafy green veggies. Even kids will devour their greens when they're in pesto form. Basil is a natural choice, of course, but it isn't always easy to come by, and truly any green makes a fantastic pesto. And although traditional pesto is made with a generous amount of extra virgin olive oil, I prefer to minimize it in my Lighter Kale Pesto Pasta (page 120), which is rich and savoury without feeling heavy.

We enjoy our red sauces, too. If you've never used lentils and walnuts to replace ground beef in your cooking, try my Bolognese-inspired Hearty Lentil-Walnut Spaghetti (page 119). It's amazing how these simple ingredients, with the right preparation and seasoning, can be transformed into something so decadent. Don't forget the Dairy-Free Pasta Topper (page 105) for this one. And for something even easier to make, try my Mushroom, Pinto Bean, and Tomato Pasta (page 116). Inspired by pasta e fagioli, I make this often when I want a simple, balanced meal that I know everyone will devour.

Dairy-Free Pasta Topper

Makes ¾ cup

A little of this savoury, Parmesan-inspired topping brings pasta nights to the next level. Parmesan cheese contains a significant amount of glutamate—that compound that we perceive as umami or savouriness. Walnuts also happen to be a rich source of glutamate, and so are my preferred nut for this recipe. Plus, they're high in plant-based omega-3 fatty acids. I'm always on the lookout for great ways to use walnuts, and this might just be my favourite.

1. Put all the ingredients in a food processor and process until a fine crumble has formed—don't overdo it or the mixture will start to become walnut butter. Store in an airtight container in the fridge for up to 2 weeks.

⅔ cup (160 mL) walnuts

¼ cup (60 mL) nutritional yeast

½ tsp (2 mL) garlic powder

¾ tsp (3 mL) salt

Variations

Other nut options: You can make dairy-free pasta topper out of pretty much any nut or seed that you like. Besides walnuts, I like almonds, pecans, and macadamia nuts in this recipe. You can also try combinations like walnut and hemp.

Shake it up: If you don't have a food processor, you can use hemp seeds in place of the walnuts and simply stir or shake the ingredients together.

Ridiculously Simple Kid Pasta

Serves 2 to 3

I don't usually make this dish for a family dinner, but rather when it's just my kids eating for some reason, like when they have an evening activity and need an early meal. The water that pasta cooks in becomes starchy, making it an excellent addition to this sauce—reserve some of that lovely cooking water to help create a smooth, lightly creamy sauce that kids devour.

1. Bring a pot of water to a boil and cook the pasta according to the package directions, reserving ½ cup (125 mL) of the pasta cooking water before draining. Return the pasta to the pot.

2. Over low heat, toss the pasta with the oil, hemp seeds, nutritional yeast, and salt. Add the pasta cooking water 1 Tbsp (15 mL) at a time until your desired consistency is reached. Taste and adjust seasonings as needed.

½ lb (225 g) short pasta, such as shells (see Tip)

1 Tbsp (15 mL) extra virgin olive oil

1 Tbsp (15 mL) hemp seeds

2 Tbsp (30 mL) nutritional yeast

½ tsp (2 mL) salt

Tip

There is some variation in the starch content of gluten-free pastas; I find that pasta made solely from rice flour tends to create especially starchy cooking water. When I'm using rice pasta in a recipe like this, where I'm using the cooking water, I either make sure to cook the pasta in plenty of water, or I dilute the starchy cooking water with plain water when adding it back into the dish.

Variation

For grown-ups: Make this more interesting for adult palates by sautéing some veggies with a pinch of dried oregano and a drizzle of balsamic vinegar, to scoop on top of the pasta.

Basic Cashew Cream Pasta

Of all the recipes in this book, this is the one that has most saved my tail. Throughout my hazy postpartum years, when energy and mental bandwidth were at all-time lows, I relied on this easy, pantry-friendly, and kid-friendly dish at least once a week. The sauce will seem on the thin side at first, but it thickens significantly when it heats up on the starchy pasta.

1. Put the cashews, water, nutritional yeast, garlic, and salt in a blender and set aside to soak while you cook the pasta.

2. Bring a pot of water to a boil and cook the pasta according to the package directions. Drain and return to the pot.

3. Meanwhile, when the pasta is almost cooked, blend the sauce ingredients on high until very smooth, 90 seconds to several minutes, pausing if the blender starts to feel hot. Pour the sauce over the pasta and heat on low on the stove until thickened and warmed through.

4. Refrigerate any leftovers in an airtight container for up to 2 to 3 days. Reheat in a saucepan over medium heat with 1 to 2 Tbsp (15 to 30 mL) water to smooth out the sauce.

1 cup (250 mL) cashews

1½ cups (375 mL) water

2 Tbsp (30 mL) nutritional yeast (optional, but adds a savoury dimension)

2 cloves garlic

1 tsp (5 mL) salt

1 lb (454 g) pasta (we like linguine)

Variations

Other nut options: Cashews make a natural heavy cream swap because they're neutral and lightly sweet. But you can sub other nuts and seeds, or a combo, if you enjoy a more assertive flavour. For example:

- Replace half of the cashews with walnuts or pecans.
- Use macadamia nuts entirely in place of cashews.
- Combine ¾ cup (185 mL) cashews with 3 Tbsp (45 mL) hemp seeds.
- Make it nut-free by using raw or toasted sunflower seeds instead of cashews.

With herbs and spices: To change up the flavour with minimal effort, add ¼ tsp (1 mL) nutmeg, 1 tsp (5 mL) fennel seed, or 1 tsp (5 mL) smoked paprika right into the sauce. When basil is in season, add a big handful of basil leaves for a creamy basil sauce that will have you licking the blender.

Make it a meal

I pair this pasta dish with at least one vegetable: frozen chopped spinach thawed and added in with the sauce; frozen peas and corn added into the pasta in the last 5 minutes of cooking; a side of steamed broccoli or green beans for when dirtying an extra pot feels okay; or a salad.

Lemon-Garlic Skillet Pasta with Cannellini Beans

Serves 4 to 6

I love this light yet creamy pasta, fragrant with fresh lemons and brown garlic, with pops of tender cannellini beans. The pasta is partially boiled, then finishes cooking in the skillet, where it soaks in the flavours of the sauce. It's perfect on hot days when a heavy tomato or cream sauce feels like too much. The white wine adds extra dimension, but it's optional—I don't always have a bottle open, and you probably don't either.

1. Check for the al dente cooking time of your pasta and subtract 3 minutes. Bring a pot of water to a boil and cook the pasta for that long, then drain it, reserving 1½ cups (375 mL) of the pasta cooking water (likely more than you'll need, but just in case). See the Tip on page 106 if you're using rice pasta.

2. Meanwhile, heat a large skillet to medium-low. Add the oil and garlic. The garlic should be calmly sizzling but not burning or sticking to the pan. Cook until the garlic is starting to gently brown, a few minutes.

3. Add the white wine, if using, and increase the heat to simmer for a few minutes to allow the alcohol to cook off.

4. Add the beans and their cooking liquid or water. Using your cooking utensil or a fork, smash up a quarter to a third of the beans to help them meld into the sauce. Add the lemon zest and juice and season with salt and pepper. Keep the sauce at a gentle simmer until you're ready to add the pasta.

5. When the pasta is ready, add it to the skillet, along with 1 cup (250 mL) of the pasta cooking water. Simmer until the pasta is fully cooked and the sauce has thickened. Add more pasta cooking water if necessary.

6. Refrigerate any leftovers in an airtight container for up to 2 to 3 days. Reheat in a saucepan over medium heat with 1 to 2 Tbsp (15 to 30 mL) water to smooth out the sauce.

1 lb (454 g) short pasta (we like medium-sized shells or rigatoni)

2 Tbsp (30 mL) extra virgin olive oil

6 cloves garlic, minced

½ cup (125 mL) white wine (optional)

2 cups (500 mL) cooked cannellini (white kidney) beans, including their cooking liquid (or sub ⅔ cup/160 mL water or stock) (see Tip on page 136)

Zest and juice of 1 lemon

Salt and pepper

Variations

With chickpeas: Use chickpeas instead of cannellini (white kidney) beans, cooking them the same way and using their cooking water.

With greens: When the pasta is nearly cooked, add to the skillet a few handfuls of finely chopped kale, arugula, or other preferred leafy green just to wilt.

Mac and Cheesy with Broccoli

Serves 4 to 6

My kids love this dairy-free mac and cheese, and honestly, so do I, especially with a big drizzle of Valentina hot sauce. (We affectionately refer to it as "mac and cheesy with broccoleesy.") Generally, it's not a good idea to put potatoes in a blender because it pulverizes the starch molecules and they can become gooey. However, in this case, that's exactly what we're going for to replicate the gooey, stretchy texture of melted cheese. No need to chop the garlic in this one because it's all going in the blender; the onion can be only coarsely chopped, for the same reason. It's small mercies like these that make some recipes feel so much more doable, isn't it?

1. Bring a pot of water to a boil and cook the pasta according to the package directions. In the last 5 minutes of cooking, add the broccoli. Drain and return to the pot.

2. Meanwhile, make the sauce by putting the potatoes, carrot, onion, garlic, cashews, and water in a medium saucepan. Bring to a boil and simmer, covered, for 12 minutes, or until the veggies are very soft. Pour the cooked vegetables, including the cooking water, into a blender along with the oil, vinegar, and salt. Blend until very smooth.

3. Pour the sauce over the pasta and broccoli, and combine well.

4. Refrigerate any leftovers in an airtight container for up to 3 days. Reheat in a saucepan over medium heat with 1 to 2 Tbsp (15 to 30 mL) water to smooth out the sauce.

1 lb (454 g) short pasta (we like elbows or shells)

1 head broccoli, chopped

1 medium russet potato, peeled and chopped into ¾-inch (2 cm) cubes

1 large carrot, scrubbed and chopped into ¾-inch (2 cm) rounds

½ cup (125 mL) chopped onion

3 cloves garlic, peeled

⅓ cup (80 mL) cashews

1½ cups (375 mL) water

2 Tbsp (30 mL) extra virgin olive oil

2 tsp (10 mL) white or rice vinegar

1 tsp (5 mL) salt

Variation

With peas: Instead of using broccoli, add 1 cup (250 mL) frozen peas to the pasta in the last 5 minutes of cooking.

Hemp Cream Rosé Penne

Serves 4 to 6

I love creamy, tangy rosé sauce, and I especially love it when it's made from nutritional powerhouse hemp seeds. Hemp seeds contain omega-3 fatty acids, vitamin E, calcium, iron, and zinc—all nutrients we want to ensure we're including in a plant-based diet. They also contain all the essential amino acids and are high in protein. On their own, hemp seeds can have a bit of a grassy flavour, but in a flavourful, garlicky rosé sauce that flavour is masked. It's easy to eat plenty of hemp seeds in this form.

1. Bring a pot of water to a boil and cook the pasta according to the package directions. Drain and return to the pot.

2. Meanwhile, heat a medium skillet over medium to medium-low heat. Add the oil and garlic and cook until the garlic has browned a little, about a minute.

3. Stir in the oregano, then add the tomatoes. Season with salt and pepper. Increase the heat to medium or medium-high and simmer vigorously until the tomatoes have started to break down, about 5 minutes.

4. Meanwhile, put the hemp seeds and water in a blender and blend until very smooth to make the hemp cream. It will seem thin at first, but it will thicken significantly once heated and simmered down. Add the hemp cream to the skillet with the tomato sauce. Simmer over medium heat until thickened, 2 to 3 minutes. Taste and season again with salt and pepper.

5. Pour the sauce over the pasta and toss to coat.

6. Refrigerate any leftovers in an airtight container for up to 2 to 3 days. Reheat in a saucepan over medium heat with 1 to 2 Tbsp (15 to 30 mL) water to smooth out the sauce.

1 lb (454 g) penne

2 to 3 tsp (10 to 15 mL) extra virgin olive oil

4 cloves garlic, minced

1½ tsp (7 mL) dried oregano

1 (14 oz/398 mL) can diced tomatoes

Salt and pepper

½ cup (125 mL) hemp seeds

1½ cups (375 mL) water

Variation

With balsamic mushrooms: Add ½ lb (225 g) chopped mushrooms along with the garlic and cook until the mushrooms release their water and soften, 3 to 5 minutes. Add 2 to 3 tsp (10 to 15 mL) balsamic vinegar. Once it is absorbed, proceed with step 3.

Mushroom, Pinto Bean, and Tomato Pasta

Serves 4 to 6

When I'm in the mood for a simple tomato-and-bean pasta, some version of this is my go-to. I've made it in vacation rentals, when we can only access canned goods and basic produce. I've made it at the peak of summer, when it's too hot to stand over the stove but we have a countertop covered in tomatoes. It doesn't require too much chopping or too many tools and always feels very easy. In a pinch, you can sub out the pintos for other beans, like romano, cannellini, or navy.

1. Bring a pot of water to a boil and cook the pasta according to the package directions. Drain and return to the pot.

2. Meanwhile, heat a large skillet or pot over medium heat. Add the oil, onion, mushrooms, and a pinch of salt. Cook until the onion is soft, the mushrooms have given up their liquid, and both are just starting to stick, 5 to 8 minutes.

3. Stir in the garlic and oregano and allow them to release their fragrance for about a minute.

4. Add the tomatoes and beans, increasing the heat to bring it up to a boil, then reduce the heat to maintain a simmer. Season with salt and pepper. Mash up some of the beans a little with the back of your stirring utensil or a fork to help them meld into the sauce. Simmer, partially covered and stirring occasionally, for 5 to 10 minutes, until the tomatoes have broken down. If you're using fresh tomatoes, you may find you need to simmer uncovered to help the sauce thicken up a little. Taste to check the seasonings, and add more salt and pepper, if needed. (You may not need to add salt if you're using canned tomatoes or beans.)

5. Pour the sauce over the cooked pasta and toss to coat.

6. Refrigerate any leftovers in an airtight container for up to 2 to 3 days. Reheat in a saucepan over medium heat with 1 to 2 Tbsp (15 to 30 mL) water to smooth out the sauce.

1 lb (454 g) small pasta (we like orecchiette or shells)

2 to 3 tsp (10 to 15 mL) extra virgin olive oil

1 medium onion, diced

8 oz (225 g) cremini mushrooms, sliced

Salt

4 cloves garlic, minced

1½ tsp (7 mL) dried oregano

3 cups (750 mL) chopped fresh tomatoes or 1 (28 oz/796 mL) can diced tomatoes

2 cups (500 mL) cooked pinto beans, drained and rinsed

Black pepper

Variations

With toasted fennel seed: I love starting this dish by frying 1½ tsp (7 mL) fennel seeds in the oil before adding the onion. This is a technique you may have seen in my Brunch Hash (page 66) and Black Bean and Tomato Soup with Toasted Fennel Seed (page 179). It adds *so* much delicious flavour for so little effort.

Mushroom and bean pasta soup: Skip cooking the pasta, and instead add ½ lb (225 g) uncooked small-type pasta when you add the beans and tomatoes to the onion and mushroom mixture, along with 6 cups (1.5 L) water or stock. Simmer, partially covered, until the pasta is cooked. It will take a few minutes longer than specified on the package because soup broth doesn't get as hot as plain water. Stir often to prevent sticking, and add more water or stock if the soup gets too thick. The soup is done with the pasta is tender.

Variation

With pecans: Use chopped pecans in place of the walnuts.

Hearty Lentil-Walnut Spaghetti

Serves 4 to 6

My kids eat big plates of this veggie-packed Bolognese-inspired pasta, and so do their parents. To create a meaty texture, a food processor is key, to get the carrots and walnuts into a ground form. And since we're getting out the food processor anyway, why not use it to chop all the ingredients to save time? Sounds good to me.

1. Bring a pot of water to a boil and cook the pasta according to the package directions. Drain and return to the pot.

2. Put the garlic cloves in a food processor and pulse to mince them. Add the onion and pulse until finely chopped.

3. Heat a large skillet or pot over medium heat. Drizzle the oil into the skillet and add the onion mixture to sauté, stirring occasionally.

4. Pulse the carrot in the food processor until a coarse meal forms. Add to the skillet, stirring to combine.

5. Pulse the mushrooms in the food processor until finely chopped. When the onion mixture looks soft, add the mushrooms to the skillet and cook until the mushrooms have released some moisture—you will see the bottom of the pan become slightly wet.

6. Pulse the walnuts in the food processor until a coarse meal forms. Add the walnuts, lentils, tomatoes, and oregano to the skillet, and bring to a simmer. Season with salt and pepper. Simmer, uncovered, for 5 to 10 minutes to soften the tomatoes and meld the flavours. If the sauce is too thick, add a splash of water; if it's too thin, keep simmering, uncovered, until it reduces.

7. Pour the sauce onto the cooked pasta and toss to coat. Alternatively, dish up the pasta and top it with the sauce.

8. Refrigerate any leftovers in an airtight container for up to 2 to 3 days. Reheat in a saucepan over medium heat with 1 to 2 Tbsp (15 to 30 mL) water to smooth out the sauce.

1 lb (454 g) spaghetti

4 cloves garlic, minced

1 medium onion

2 to 3 tsp (10 to 15 mL) extra virgin olive oil

1 medium carrot, scrubbed and chopped into 1- to 2-inch (2.5 to 5 cm) chunks

6 oz (170 g) cremini mushrooms

1 cup (250 mL) walnuts

1½ cups (375 mL) cooked brown or green lentils, drained and rinsed if canned (see Tip)

1 (28 oz/796 mL) can diced or crushed tomatoes

1½ tsp (7 mL) dried oregano

Salt and pepper

Tip

To cook the lentils from dried, add ½ cup (125 mL) rinsed dried lentils to a small saucepan with 1½ cups (375 mL) water. Bring to a boil and simmer, covered, until the lentils are tender, about 20 minutes. Drain.

Lighter Kale Pesto Pasta

Serves 4 to 5

I love a basil pesto, but quality basil can be hard to find for most of the year. This kale version satisfies my pesto craving even in the deepest of winter. I also turn to pesto often in the spring, when I'm inspired by the abundance of fresh greens. Traditional pesto relies on Parmesan for a hit of savoury and salty. Here, we use a triple hit of umami-rich ingredients to replicate that: walnuts, nutritional yeast, and miso (the miso also lends saltiness).

1. Bring a pot of water to a boil and cook the pasta according to the package directions, reserving 1 cup (250 mL) of the pasta cooking water before draining (see Tip on page 106). Drain and return to the pot.

2. In a food processor, add the kale, walnuts, oil, miso, garlic, and nutritional yeast. Process until a thick, even paste forms.

3. Add the pesto to the pasta and slowly add the reserved pasta cooking water, stirring, until you reach a smooth consistency. You probably won't need quite the full reserved amount. Season with salt and pepper.

4. Refrigerate any leftovers in an airtight container for up to 2 to 3 days. Reheat in a saucepan over medium heat with 1 to 2 Tbsp (15 to 30 mL) water to smooth out the sauce.

1 lb (454 g) long or short pasta (we like linguine or rotini)

3 gently packed cups (750 mL) destemmed and torn kale leaves (about 2 oz/60 g)

⅔ cup (160 mL) walnut halves

3 Tbsp (45 mL) extra virgin olive oil

1 Tbsp (15 mL) white miso

2 cloves garlic

¼ cup (60 mL) nutritional yeast

Salt and pepper

Variations

With basil: In the summer, when gorgeous bunches of basil are everywhere, use that in place of 1 to 2 cups (250 to 500 mL) of the kale.

With white beans: Add 1½ cups rinsed white beans to the food processor in step 2. This results in a creamier, heartier pesto that's packed with bean goodness.

Make it nut-free: Try using ½ cup (125 mL) raw or toasted pumpkin seeds in place of the walnuts. This is a great option if you're allergic to nuts, and if not, it's simply a delicious variation.

Bowl Tuesday

Bowls are the plant-based answer to meat and potatoes, that basic formula that can grace your dinner plate infinite ways. Rather than protein, starch, and veg, the bowl formula is this: grain or starch, legume, veggies, sauce, and toppings.

Bowls are really family-friendly because they're so customizable. Although as a rule I don't cook separate dinners for the kids, I feel comfortable with plating up all our bowls differently, according to our needs and tastes. Arden and I generally get way more leafy greens. If the kids aren't into the toasted nut I'm offering, they can get a sprinkle of neutral hemp seeds instead. I always serve up a little scoop of everything to the kids, though—you never know when someone will suddenly, inexplicably, start loving something, because kids be kids.

Components of bowls scale up easily, and since they're building blocks, they can be used for future meals in various ways. So, if I'm cooking rice, I'll make a giant pot, with an eye to making Healthier Fried Brown Rice (page 198) another day and maybe Brown Rice Nori Rolls (page 96), too. When I make Saucy Simple Mexican-Inspired Beans (page 136), I fill my biggest skillet, doubling or tripling the recipe. Not only do these beans make great leftovers for lunchtime bowls—packed or at home—they're perfect repurposed in tacos. I'm always grateful to have prepared Cabbage Slaw (page 151) in the fridge as well, to scoop onto bowls, salads, tacos, and sandwiches.

Having bowls on Tuesdays—early in the week—works well because it's a chance to ensure the fridge is stocked with these versatile meal components. This makes the rest of our week go more smoothly and feel less frazzled. After an easy pasta night on Monday, I'm ready to spend a few extra minutes on Tuesday prepping the ingredients we can lean on over the rest of the week when the hungries strike.

This chapter is laid out a little differently than the other chapters, to empha-size the build-a-bowl nature of this style of eating. Rather than giving you bowl recipes, I lay out the elements of a bowl component by component. At the end of the chapter (page 161), you'll find suggested bowl combinations—but I hope you will use the components as inspiration to make your own customized bowls.

How to Make a Bowl

My basic formula for making bowls is this:

- 1 grain or starch
- 1 legume
- At least 1 veggie, sometimes 2 or 3
- Sauce
- Toppings

The grain or starch, legume, and veggies make up the heart of the bowl. The sauce contributes flavour and moisture, though sometimes I'll skip the sauce if the main components have enough moisture—say, if I'm making saucy pinto beans with well-dressed slaw. The toppings—for example, nuts, seeds, sauerkraut—add texture and nutrition, in addition to yet more flavour.

At dinnertime, I generally have the capacity to put some effort into one or two of the bowl ingredients, but no more. For example, if I'm making marinated lentils and toasted walnuts, I'm probably not also roasting potatoes, making a complicated salad, and blending a sauce. Instead, I'd pair those lentils and walnuts with plain quinoa or rice, and add some chopped greens simply dressed with olive oil and lemon juice or vinegar.

In the pages that follow, I go into detail on all these components and suggest many ingredients and combinations. But even if you're pressed for time or mental bandwidth, follow my simple formula—grain/starch, legume, veggie(s), sauce, toppings—to create a beautiful, nutritious meal. For example, cook a pot of quinoa, drain a can of chickpeas, add a handful of greens, drizzle with extra virgin olive oil and red wine vinegar, and top with slivered almonds and olives. Boom, dinner is ready, maybe even with leftovers for lunch tomorrow.

You can also think regional when coming up with bowl combinations. My personal all-time fave is the Mediterranean combination of olive oil, lemon juice, and garlic. For me, this flavour profile conjures up creamy white beans, bitter-crisp greens, briny olives and capers, and handfuls of parsley. And you can never go wrong with a Mexican-inspired meal. If you've got beans and limes, you've got the beginnings of a delicious meal. Cook up rice or potatoes, toss in some chopped greens, add salsa or guacamole, and dinner is served.

When creating your own bowls, keep in mind the Flavour Fundamentals (page 31):

- You may want a little something **acidic**, which can come from the sauce or can be as simple as a squeeze of lemon or lime juice over top.
- Consider adding an **umami-rich** ingredient, such as mushrooms, tomatoes, soy sauce, walnuts, or browned ingredients, like pan-fried tofu, roasted root veggies, or toasted nuts and seeds.
- Try to incorporate some **texture**—something you can sink your teeth into, or something crunchy.
- Don't forget the **salt**.

Grains and Other Bases

Generally, I like to start my bowls with a plain whole grain, such as brown rice or quinoa. I also love and often eat polenta, ever since I discovered it can be made quickly and easily in my pressure cooker (thank you, Internet). If I have a little extra energy and time for chopping and/or baking, I'll roast or bake potatoes as well. We also like soba noodles, cooked according to the package directions—they're especially good with tofu and tempeh. And don't forget about bread or toast as a delicious bowl base. For those who aren't gluten-free, grains like barley and farro are a wonderful option. This is a quick primer on bowl bases and how to cook them:

Brown Rice

We prefer brown jasmine rice, which is much softer than any other brown rice I've tried, and it's extra palatable to kids. It cooks more quickly, too, in about 25 minutes. (This rice also works great for Brown Rice Nori Rolls, page 96.) Rice is rendered more nutritious both following a period of soaking and being cooked like pasta, in extra water and then drained. If I think of it, I'll start my rice soaking in the morning or during the day. Rinse the rice in a sieve, add it to a pot with plenty of water and set aside to soak. At cooking time, drain and rinse the rice, and add back into a large pot. Cover with a generous amount of water, ideally 3 to 4 inches (8 to 10 cm). Cook until tender, 20 to 25 minutes for brown jasmine rice, 40 to 50 minutes for other brown rice varieties. Drain any excess water. Store any leftovers in an airtight container for 4 to 6 days in the fridge or up to 6 months in the freezer.

Quinoa

For fluffy quinoa, I use a 1:1.5 ratio of quinoa to water. Cover, bring to a boil, then reduce to a gentle simmer. Allow to simmer, covered, for 10 minutes, at which point the water should be absorbed (if not, simmer for another couple of minutes). Without lifting the lid, remove the pot from the heat and let steam for another 5 minutes before fluffing with a fork. Store any leftovers in an airtight container for up to 4 to 6 days in the fridge and up to 6 months in the freezer.

Polenta

Polenta—essentially corn meal porridge—is one of my favourite grain bases. It's creamy, faintly sweet, and never dry. You can serve polenta two basic ways: When it's freshly cooked and still pourable, simply dish it up and top with your ingredients. Or, after it has firmed up, slice and fry or bake it with a little oil until crispy. Both versions are wonderful. If you'd like to soften up leftover polenta, put it in a pot over medium heat, and whisk in water slowly until your desired consistency is attained.

You can make polenta with virtually any corn meal that's coarser than corn flour—it doesn't need to be labelled as polenta, so don't worry about stocking both corn meal *and* polenta meal in your pantry. It's a myth that you need to carefully whisk polenta into boiling water with esoteric skill. Adding it to cold water and whisking it like a normal person is fine.

Pressure cooker method: In a pressure cooker, combine 1 part coarsely ground corn meal or polenta meal with 4 parts water (in my experience, it must be coarsely ground in pressure cookers because finely ground has a tendency to stick). Season with salt and pepper. Set to 9 minutes at high pressure. When it's done, manually release the pressure, then give the polenta a good whisk to fully combine it and lift any stuck bits from the bottom of the cooker. Add a little olive oil or vegan butter, if you'd like.

Stovetop method: In a saucepan, combine 1 part corn meal or polenta meal with 5 parts water. Season with salt and pepper. Over medium heat, bring to a simmer, then reduce the heat to low to keep the simmer gentle. Whisk often and change to a spoon once the mixture becomes too thick to whisk, stirring every few minutes until the polenta is thickened and tender and the raw taste is cooked off, 30 to 45 minutes. Finish by adding a little olive oil or vegan butter, if you'd like.

For either method: Pour any polenta that doesn't get used right away into a baking dish, sheet pan, or food storage container with a flat bottom, and smooth the top. Store in an airtight container in the fridge for up to 4 to 6 days. When ready to use, slice it and fry it on both sides in a little extra virgin olive oil until crisping and warmed through.

Admittedly, stovetop polenta can feel a bit ambitious. There's zero shame in using prepared polenta, though it often has additives that can negatively impact the flavour. Experiment for yourself and see what you like.

Potatoes and Sweet Potatoes

I love potatoes. Who doesn't? Endlessly versatile and nutritious, potatoes make a perfect bowl base that will please just about everyone. Once cooked, refrigerate leftovers in an airtight container for up to 5 days.

For boiled potatoes: Ideally start with a lower-starch potato—like Yukon gold, fingerling, or new potatoes—so they don't fall apart. Cut into uniform pieces or leave whole, depending on how big they are and your personal preference. Add into a saucepan and cover with cold water by about 1 inch (2.5 cm). Boil, uncovered, until fork-tender, about 10 minutes.

For mashed potatoes: For maximum fluff, start with a starchy potato, like russet. Most people seem to prefer them peeled, but sometimes it's a nice change to leave the skin on. Chop into uniform pieces, submerge in cold water by about 1 inch (2.5 cm), and simmer uncovered until very soft, about 10 minutes—or a little more for good measure. Drain and return to the pot. Add a dollop of vegan butter and a sprinkle of salt and mash up a bit. Add splashes of unsweetened plant-based milk and keep mashing until your desired consistency is reached. You can also make mashed sweet potatoes—they will need very little plant milk, if any, because they are quite moist after boiling.

For roasted potatoes: Scrub and cube virtually any regular or sweet potato—peeled or not—into uniform bite-sized pieces, toss in a bowl with extra virgin olive oil and salt to lightly coat, and then spread evenly on a baking sheet. I roast potatoes at 400°F (200°C) for the simple reason that it's below my olive oil's smoke point (see page 7 for more on oil smoke points). Use your oven's convection setting if it has one for drier heat that browns faster with less stickage. Cook the potatoes in the preheated oven until browned and fork-tender, 35 to 40 minutes, turning after 20 minutes. Roasting at 425°F (220°C) or 450°F (230°C) will speed things up and result in crispier, drier potatoes—use avocado oil, though, to prevent the oil burning, and start checking for doneness at 25 minutes. To make smoky roasted potatoes, season generously with smoked paprika along with the salt.

Alternatively, for sweet potatoes, scrub them and pat dry, cut in half lengthwise, oil lightly, place cut side down on a baking sheet, and sprinkle with salt. Roast at 400°F (200°C) until a knife goes in easily, 30 to 35 minutes, depending on how big they are.

Roasted sweet potatoes tend to keep well; roasted regular potatoes, less so. I often bake up a full tray of halved sweet potatoes to have them in the fridge throughout the week—if they last that long!

For baked potatoes: Start with fairly uniformly sized russet potatoes. Wash then pat dry, pierce with a fork, rub lightly with olive oil, and sprinkle with salt. For best results, bake at 350°F (175°C) directly on the oven rack until a sharp knife goes through the thickest part of a test potato without resistance, about an hour or a little more.

Legumes

Undeniably, the easiest way to add legumes to a bowl is plain. Canned or cooked beans, rinsed, are delicious on their own; I often have chickpeas and beans this way on my lunchtime salads and bowls. Frozen edamame can be dished up after only a 4-minute steam. However, a little extra effort if you're up for it can transform legumes—they easily absorb flavour and are a perfect vehicle for aromatics, spices, acids, and/or salt.

If I have Oil-Free Hummus (page 214) or White Bean Purée (page 215) in the fridge, I'll often use these in bowls, too. It's such an easy way to add flavour and moistures. Roasted potatoes and cauliflower go so well with hummus and an extra squeeze of lemon juice, and I love quinoa with kale salad or steamed broccoli and a big scoop of white bean purée.

Beans: How to cook from dried

I'm not above using canned beans, and I try to keep a few cans in my cupboards at all times—types we tend to use in smaller amounts or can't find dried, or our fave kinds for when we need a quick bean fix.

But there's no denying that for flavour and price, you can't beat beans cooked from dried. Plus, the lovely starchy water they've cooked in is flavourful and creamy, and is itself a great addition to many dishes. A big container of tender chickpeas, or pinto or cannellini beans, in the fridge or freezer can inspire so many meals throughout the week, including soups, bowls, pastas, tacos, and straight-up bean sautés.

I know that cooking beans from dried can seem like a hassle, and that's largely because for a single meal it feels like too much planning and effort—which, frankly, it is. That's why I always cook beans in big batches. Generally, I cook 2 pounds (900 grams) of dried beans or chickpeas, divide it into four portions, keep one or two in the fridge, and freeze the rest. When the freezer stash is running low, I'll cook up more, loosely rotating through my favourites (black, pinto, cannellini, and chickpea). That way, there's usually a stockpile of something ready to go, and I never have to plan ahead for a particular meal, which I'm pretty sure I'm constitutionally incapable of.

Aside from requiring some time, cooking beans from dried is actually very easy and hands-off. In my experience, there are two ways the process can go wrong, both entirely avoidable:

1. Very old dried beans are at risk of being tough and never fully softening. If you've had beans sitting in your cupboard for a few years, compost them and start fresh.

2. Adding an acidic ingredient to the pot while the beans are cooking can make them take longer to cook, or in extreme cases, prevent them from fully softening. Avoid adding tomatoes, vinegar, citrus, or any other acidic ingredient to your beans before they're fully cooked, at least until you get the hang of cooking beans from dried and you're ready to experiment with cooking beans in mildly acidic mediums (it is a thing—baked beans is one example).

Once you've got your hands on some non-ancient beans, here's what to do:

Soak 'em. It's important to soak dried beans to improve their digestibility and nutrient availability. Rinse beans in a colander to clean them, then put in a pot. Cover with plenty of cold water—the beans will expand, so be sure to cover them by a good 3 to 4 inches (8 to 10 cm). Leave them to soak for anywhere from 5 to 24 hours; any longer and the beans may start to ferment or sprout.

Rinse and replace. Drain and then rinse the beans again. Return them to the pot and cover with fresh water by about a scant inch (about 2 cm) for a pressure cooker, or by a couple of inches (5 cm) for the stovetop. It's a myth that salting the cooking water toughens the beans. In fact, salting the cooking water is a great way to infuse flavour right into the beans. Go ahead and salt the water a little, if you'd like. I typically add 1 tsp (5 mL) of salt per 1 lb (454 g) of beans. This is also a fine time to add a little onion or dried herbs that benefit from a long cook, like bay leaves or oregano—but this is totally optional.

Simmer until tender. Short version: just literally simmer . . . until tender. You can do this either on the stove top or in the pressure cooker.

Stovetop method

Cover the pot with a lid, bring the beans to a boil, and then reduce the heat to a gentle simmer. Simmer, covered, until beans are tender, monitoring to ensure the beans are submerged in water, and adding more water if needed.

The cooking time will vary depending on the age and type of your beans, and on how tender you like them (I like them on the soft side). Just keep an eye on them and start tasting for doneness after about 1 hour. Give the beans a stir, and scoop out at least two beans to bite into—like pasta, they should be easy to bite through but not mushy. If the beans are *undercooked*, continue to simmer them. If they're *overcooked*, make bean purée or soup with them. I have both undercooked and overcooked beans in my many years of cooking them. It's not a big deal—it will happen and you will recover. Don't let the fear of failure prevent you from trying!

Pressure cooker method

Set to high pressure and set the time. Cooking times will vary according to factors like the age of the beans as well as your personal preference. You can consult your pressure cooker manual for the manufacturer's recommended cook times, or use the times listed below for the beans called for in this book's recipes. Remember, these times are for soaked beans:

- Black beans: 4 to 6 minutes
- Cannellini (white kidney) beans: 5 to 7 minutes
- Chickpeas: 12 to 14 minutes
- Pinto beans: 4 to 6 minutes

Choose the lower end of the range if you're cooking beans that you know aren't very old, and/or if you want the beans to be on the firmer side for sautés or salads. Choose the higher end of the range if you're cooking with older beans, and/or if you want softer beans for soups or purées, or to mash (e.g., for Saucy Simple Mexican-Inspired Beans, page 136, or Chickpea Salad Sandwiches, page 88). Use the middle of the range if you're unsure and intimidated by all this, just so that you can get your feet wet and realize that cooking beans in a pressure cooker is actually quite easy and forgiving.

Let the pressure come down naturally to prevent the beans from bursting. Sometimes I cheat this a little and release the pressure after it has mostly come down naturally, after about 15 minutes.

Eat or store. Use immediately, or portion the beans and their cooking liquid into containers. If you put them in the fridge, they will firm up a little and the starchy water they cooked in will become thicker and creamier. They'll keep for up to 3 to 4 days, or a day or two longer if they've been salted. Or you can freeze the beans for up to 6 months.

Saucy Simple Mexican-Inspired Beans

Serves 4 to 6

Saucy seasoned pinto or black beans are a major staple in my household. Paired with a grain or starch and a steamed veggie or salad, you have a complete meal without too much effort. Leftover beans, which tend to firm up, are also ideal for tacos. With a straightforward flavour and creamy texture, these delicious beans are also very kid-friendly.

The creaminess of the beans comes partially from the beans themselves, slightly mashed, and partially from the starchy water the beans cook in. When you first add the beans and liquid, the mixture will seem too thin, but it reduces a little upon simmering, thickens with a bit of a mash, and then thickens further upon cooling. I'm always surprised by how much it thickens up as it cools.

1. Heat a skillet over medium heat. Add the oil, then cumin and coriander. Toast the spices for a few seconds until they start to brown and smell fragrant.

2. Add the beans, along with their cooking liquid, onion powder, and garlic powder. Season with salt (how much you'll need depends on whether the beans were salted to begin with and your personal preference).

3. Simmer for 5 to 10 minutes, mashing up some of the beans with a fork, to combine flavours and thicken the sauce. Add another ½ cup (125 mL) bean cooking liquid or water if needed to maintain a glossy, smooth consistency—the beans should not appear dry or stiff. The beans will thicken further as they cool.

4. Refrigerate any leftovers in an airtight container for 3 to 5 days.

2 to 3 tsp (10 to 15 mL) oil

1 tsp (5 mL) cumin

2 tsp (10 mL) ground coriander

4 cups (1 L) cooked black or pinto beans, plus the cooking liquid they're submerged in (or sub 1⅓ cups/330 mL water or stock) (see Tip)

1 tsp (5 mL) onion powder

1½ tsp (7 mL) garlic powder

Salt

Make it a meal

These beans naturally pair with rice, potatoes, sweet potatoes, or tortillas. My go-to veggies to have with these are Cabbage Slaw (page 151) and Avocado-Rubbed Kale (page 151). When I have extra energy, I also like to add Seared Peppers and Onions (page 148), which makes my kitchen smell amazing. Also try them with tangy quick-pickled red cabbage (page 152). The beans are quite saucy on their own, but they're also delicious topped with Cilantro-Lime Cream (page 155) or Super Speedy Salsa (page 155).

Tip

You can substitute canned beans, if you'd like.
Either choose canned beans that do not contain
added preservatives, like disodium EDTA or calcium
chloride, so that you can use the liquid in the can.
Or rinse your canned beans and then substitute
plain water or stock for the bean cooking liquid—it
won't be quite as creamy, but it will still be delicious.

Lemon-Garlic Cannellini Beans

Serves 4

These beans come together quickly but are very flavourful. I use cannellini (white kidney) beans because they're absolutely delicious and widely available where I live, but other large white beans—like canary, peruano, great northern, or butter—work, too. I can never resist the pungent, zesty aroma of garlic and lemon cooking together, and their flavours pair so perfectly with creamy white beans.

1. Heat a medium skillet over medium heat. Add the oil and garlic and sauté until the garlic is just starting to turn brown, 1 to 2 minutes.

2. Stir in the beans. Cook until warmed through, another minute.

3. Stir in the lemon zest and juice, and season with salt and pepper. The lemon juice should help lift up any stuck garlic bits from the bottom of the pan. If the mixture still looks dry or stuck, add bean cooking liquid (or water) 1 Tbsp (15 mL) at a time until a smooth consistency is reached.

4. Refrigerate any leftovers in an airtight container for 3 to 5 days.

2 to 3 tsp (10 to 15 mL) extra virgin olive oil

4 cloves garlic, minced

2 cups (500 mL) cooked cannellini beans, drained, 2 Tbsp (30 mL) cooking liquid reserved

Zest and juice of 1 lemon (skip the zest if you just cannot right now)

Salt and pepper

Make it a meal

These versatile beans go with so many grains and starches: brown rice, quinoa, polenta, potatoes, sweet potatoes, and even simply toast. Try them with a simple green salad, perhaps dressed in Everyday Vinaigrette (page 76). They also go well with Garlic-Wilted Spring Greens (page 147), Roasted Asparagus (page 148), Lemony Arugula and Herbs (page 148), Blackened Broccoli (page 148), Blistered Cherry Tomatoes with Garlic and Basil (page 151), Grated Carrot Salad (page 151), and Roasted Root Veggies (page 147), and quick-pickled onions (page 152). They're saucy enough on their own—or try a smear of Fresh Herb Purée (page 156) on the plate to take it to the next level.

Variation

With greens: Add a handful of chopped spinach, kale, chard, or whatever other greens you like along with the lemon juice. They should just soften and wilt.

Lentils in Garlicky Red Wine Vinaigrette

Serves 4 to 6

These tangy, garlicky lentils pack a serious flavour punch. I love to have them on hand to add to bowls and salads throughout the week—they only become more flavourful the longer they marinate. When I posted an earlier version of these online, many people wrote to me to say they had become a regular dish in their weekly meal-prep routines.

1. Put the lentils in a pot along with 4 cups (1 L) water. Cover, bring to a boil, then reduce to a simmer. Simmer the lentils for 20 to 25 minutes, or until they're tender. Drain well.

2. Meanwhile, in a large bowl, whisk together the oil, vinegar, lemon juice, garlic, mustard, maple syrup, and salt.

3. Add the cooked lentils to the bowl and toss with the vinaigrette to coat. Leave on the counter to marinate for at least 15 minutes before serving, if you can, stirring once or twice while they sit.

4. Refrigerate any leftovers in an airtight container for 5 to 7 days.

1⅓ cups (330 mL) French, brown, or green lentils, rinsed (see Tip)

3 Tbsp (45 mL) extra virgin olive oil

3 Tbsp (45 mL) red wine vinegar

Juice of 1 lemon

3 cloves garlic, minced

2 tsp (10 mL) Dijon mustard

2 tsp (10 mL) pure maple syrup

½ tsp (2 mL) salt

Tip
Brown and green lentils are the most common dried lentils I see in grocery stores. They're a wonderful, accessible option. But my personal favourite is French lentils, which have a firm texture and peppery bite.

Make it a meal
Try these delicious lentils with quinoa, potatoes, or toast. Since they're tangy, they also go great with polenta and sweet potatoes, which provide contrasting sweetness. Add a crisp green salad, Grated Carrot Salad (page 151), Lemony Arugula and Herbs (page 148), Blackened Broccoli (page 148), Roasted Root Veggies (page 147), or Umami-Bomb Mushrooms (page 151).

Five-Minute Paprika-Spiked Chickpeas and Greens

Serves 4

So simple, so delicious. These chickpeas couldn't be easier, and they're a great addition to just about any weeknight bowl. You can also try this on a slice of toast for an easy lunch. I find the aroma from the sautéing paprika and garlic powder intoxicating, and the spices really transform the chickpeas.

1. Heat a wide skillet over medium heat. Add the oil and swirl it around in the pan. Stir in the chickpeas, kale, paprika, and garlic powder, and season with salt and pepper.

2. Drizzle in the water and sauté the mixture until the greens wilt and the chickpeas are warmed through. Add more water if needed to maintain a smooth consistency and glossy appearance—it should not look dry.

2 to 3 tsp (10 to 15 mL) extra virgin olive oil

2 cups (500 mL) cooked chickpeas, drained and rinsed

3 big kale or collard leaves, finely chopped

2 tsp (10 mL) sweet paprika

1 tsp (5 mL) garlic powder

Salt and pepper

1 Tbsp (15 mL) water

Make it a meal

You could enjoy these with just about any grain or starch, but I especially like them with potatoes, sweet potatoes, or toast. They're also wonderful on polenta. Since this dish already contains a vegetable, you could consider it complete, or add Lemony Arugula and Herbs (page 148) and quick-pickled onions (page 152). My simple Tahini-Lemon Sauce (page 155) is great drizzled on top.

Savoury Pan-Crisped Tofu Cubes

Serves 4

These simple, delicious tofu cubes are a fave of my kids. I like that they take mere minutes to make and require only a few ingredients. Everyone wins! Make sure to double the recipe if you'd like to have extra on hand for lunches and snacks.

1. Preheat a skillet over medium-high heat.

2. Drain and rinse the tofu, then pat dry with a clean tea towel. Cut into bite-sized cubes.

3. Add the oil then tofu to the skillet, shaking the pan to spread out the cubes. Keep shaking the pan every minute or so, using a flipper to turn over the cubes if necessary so they brown on several sides.

4. When the cubes are browned on most sides, add the soy sauce— careful, it will spatter a bit. Keep moving the tofu around until the soy sauce is absorbed and the cubes look deeply golden and matte (rather than still wet).

5. Refrigerate leftovers in an airtight container for 4 to 5 days.

1 (12 oz/350 g) block extra-firm tofu

1 Tbsp (15 mL) avocado oil

2 Tbsp (30 mL) soy sauce

Make it a meal

These tofu cubes are especially good on rice, soba noodles, and even mashed potatoes. Try them with Blackened Broccoli (page 148) and Umami-Bomb Mushrooms (page 151). I love to drizzle Citrus-Hemp Sauce (page 155) on these; if you're going the mashed potato route, definitely make some Nearly Instant Gravy (page 156) to accompany them.

Sheet Pan Chickpeas and Cauliflower

Serves 4 to 6

Even just hearing the words "sheet pan dinner" makes me feel more relaxed. There's something appealing about dinner getting flavourful and delicious on a single pan in the oven while you do something else. Roasting chickpeas produces a hearty, chewy texture. And roasted cauliflower is one of life's great blessings, juicy and crisp with plenty of flavour. I adore this easy and delicious dish.

1. Preheat the oven to 375°F (190°C).

2. In a large mixing bowl, combine all the ingredients, stirring to mix well.

3. Spread on a large baking sheet, arranging the cauliflower florets so they are mostly cut side down.

4. Roast until cauliflower is fork-tender to your liking, about 30 minutes.

5. Refrigerate any leftovers in an airtight container for up to 3 to 5 days.

3 cups (750 mL) cooked chickpeas, drained, rinsed, and patted dry with a tea towel

1 medium cauliflower, cut into bite-sized florets (about 1½ lb/675 g of florets)

4 to 5 cloves garlic, coarsely chopped (not minced)

2 Tbsp (30 mL) extra virgin olive oil

2 tsp (10 mL) sweet paprika

¾ tsp (3 mL) salt

Make it a meal

Since you have the oven on, why not roast some potatoes or sweet potatoes, while you're at it? They're fantastic with this dish. I also love these toasty chickpeas and cauliflower on a bed of creamy polenta or easy quinoa. Add Lemony Arugula and Herbs (page 148) or quick-pickled onions (page 152), if you'd like, but since the vegetable is included in the recipe, it's not essential. I love a big drizzle of Tahini-Lemon Sauce (page 155) on this.

Veggies

There are basically four ways I prepare vegetables for bowls:

- **Roasting:** Creates a crisp brown exterior that boosts flavour.
- **Steaming:** Fast and easy, and results in moist, soft veggies that are easy to eat, especially for kids.
- **Sautéing:** Also fast, and a good way to quickly cook more tender veggies that don't necessarily need to be cooked through in a hot oven.
- **Raw:** Crisp and refreshing, they often provide textural interest. Many raw veggies, like cabbage and carrots, are especially good shredded, which makes them easier to chew and increases their surface area and thus their flavour potential.

I rarely boil vegetables because it leaches water-soluble nutrients from them into the cooking water.

There's no one right way of doing things. Some people prefer very soft steamed veggies, while others prefer them crisp. In the summer you might crave crunchy, cool salads, while in the winter you're happiest digging into a pan of roasted root veggies. If you like it, it's good.

Here are a few of my go-to ways to prepare veggies through the seasons. I've opted to share loose recipes here, rather than specifying quantities, to emphasize how important it is to work with what you've got and what you like—a big theme in how I approach cooking. Vegetables are diverse and delicious. Whether you add one clove of garlic or six, the result will be wonderful—one version will simply be more garlicky, and both have their time and place.

Roasted Root Veggies

Roasting root veggies mellows their flavour, amplifies their sweetness, and introduces those tasty, tasty brown edges. Preheat your oven to 400°F (200°C). Use the convection setting if you have one—the fan keeps the oven extra dry, resulting in browner veggies in less time. Scrub or peel two or three kinds of root veggies—like beet, carrot, parsnip, turnip, sweet potato, and/or onion—and chop into uniform bite-sized pieces. Winter squashes and fennel bulbs work well here, too. Toss with oil, salt, and pepper. Spread evenly on a baking sheet, taking care not to crowd, and roast until browning and tender. Root veggies can take 40 to 60 minutes, depending on how large your pieces are, how many you're roasting, and your doneness preference. Give them a flip every 15 to 20 minutes. Toss in some rinsed chickpeas 20 minutes before the cooking time is up to make it a sheet pan meal.

Garlic-Wilted Spring Greens

One of my favourite parts about spring, besides the singing birds, warming days, and new life everywhere (um, actually I like everything about spring), is the enormous variety of tender greens that floods gardens and markets. My friend Zach jokes that wilting greens is my signature move, and he's not wrong, especially in spring. You only need garlic, olive oil, and a quick trip to a pan to transform greens into so much more than the sum of their parts. Some of my top picks are kale flowers, fava bean tips, sorrel, tatsoi, arugula, and watercress, and of course good ol' spinach—but this will vary for you depending on what you have access to.

To make garlic-wilted greens, simply heat a pan over medium heat, swirl in a small amount of extra virgin olive oil, and add a few cloves of minced garlic. When fragrant, stir in a few handfuls of up to three types of mixed spring greens and then immediately turn off the heat while turning the greens—they will wilt simply from contact with the hot oil and pan. Seriously, leafy greens wilt quickly, and this is doubly true with young spring greens, so don't be shy about turning off that heat. You can always turn it back on. Enjoy right away if you can, refrigerating any leftovers in an airtight container for up to 3 days.

Roasted Asparagus

If you've never tried roasting asparagus, I can't recommend it highly enough. Preheat the oven to 400°F (200°C). Clean the asparagus and snap off the tough, woody ends. Toss the asparagus with a little oil and salt, spread on a baking sheet, and roast until browning and tender to your liking, 10 to 20 minutes, depending on how thick the asparagus is and how soft you like it.

Lemony Arugula and Herbs

This is one of those dishes that has so much more flavour than you'd expect considering how simple it is. Combine a few handfuls of arugula with a handful each of two or three different chopped fresh herbs. Parsley, cilantro, basil, and mint are all great choices, or use whatever you happen to like. Add a drizzle of extra virgin olive oil, a squeeze of lemon juice, a sprinkle of salt, and a few grinds of black pepper, and toss to coat. Taste and adjust flavours to your liking and enjoy right away.

Seared Peppers and Onions

Seared peppers and onions—essentially, fajita veggies—pair well with Mexican dishes. Bonus: they make your kitchen smell amazing, and leftovers are perfect for tacos. Thinly slice green bell peppers and onions. Heat a pan over medium-high heat, swirl in a little avocado oil, and add the peppers and onion. They will blacken and blister—this is what you want. Stirring often, cook for about 10 minutes, or until veggies are darkened and soft. Refrigerate any leftovers for 3 to 5 days

Blackened Broccoli

My kids love steamed broccoli tossed with a little vegan butter or extra virgin olive oil, and so do I. But for something with a little more flavour and to keep things interesting, this blackened broccoli is a go-to. You can't really taste the soy sauce—it just adds some saltiness and depth—making this is a versatile broccoli option.

To make, cut a head of broccoli into smallish florets. Heat a pan (ideally cast iron) over medium-high heat, swirl in a little avocado oil, then add the florets. They will start to blacken over the high heat. Turn them a few times to get dark spots on a few sides, then drizzle in a little soy sauce and a splash of water—it will sizzle. Cover the pan with a lid and allow the broccoli to steam for about 5 minutes, or until tender. Refrigerate any leftovers for 3 to 5 days.

Blistered Cherry Tomatoes with Garlic and Basil

We grow tomatoes, and inevitably there's a glorious period in late summer when we're swimming in more tomatoes than we can eat. That's when I'll often heat a skillet over medium heat, swirl in a little extra virgin olive oil, and toss in a few handfuls of cherry tomatoes. Let them brown a little on a few sides. When they've started to break down, add some chopped garlic and salt. Mash the tomatoes up a little with the back of your spoon, if you'd like to make them saucier, and for the satisfaction of feeling them burst. Stir in finely chopped fresh basil, if you'd like, and dish into your bowls. This also goes well on pasta or toast. Refrigerate any leftovers for 3 to 5 days.

Avocado-Rubbed Kale

Massaging kale with acid and/or salt breaks down some of its cell walls, making it more tender and a better vehicle for flavour. Creamy, fatty avocado is a perfect companion for this process. Slice the kale into thin strips. (Kale is hearty, and big pieces are too difficult to eat.) Put it in a bowl along with chunks of avocado, a drizzle of red wine vinegar (or other acid), and a sprinkle of salt. Use your clean hands to massage the ingredients together until the kale is coated, softened, and reduced in volume slightly.

Grated Carrot Salad

In France, this is a popular way to enjoy carrots. Grating carrots roughens their edges and increases their surface area, so they absorb flavour and feel easy to eat. Scrub or peel carrots, grate, and toss with a little olive oil, freshly squeezed lemon juice, and salt. As with all slaw-style salads, the flavour will improve upon sitting for even just 10 or 15 minutes. This salad keeps well in the fridge for up to 5 days. Serve at room temperature.

Umami-Bomb Mushrooms

These intensely delicious mushrooms can be used almost like a relish or pickle, as a condiment to provide a hit of flavour on the side. I like shiitake mushrooms, but this method works with any mushroom. Cook sliced mushrooms with a small amount of oil in a skillet over medium heat until browning. Avoid salting. When the mushrooms start to stick, add a drizzle each of balsamic vinegar and soy sauce, and cook until the liquid evaporates and the mushrooms are juicy and tender, and coated in a glistening sauce. The combination of mushrooms, the Maillard reaction, balsamic vinegar, and soy sauce is a serious umami bomb.

Cabbage Slaw

This is a year-round staple in my kitchen. It's yummy and nutritious, it doesn't require cooking, and it pairs well with so many dishes. Finely shred a chunk of red or green cabbage using a sharp knife or mandoline. You want the slices to be as thin as you can make them, and no more than a couple of inches (5 cm) long—we're not making noodles here. Use a fork to mix in a dollop of vegan mayo or a drizzle of extra virgin olive oil, a drizzle of acid (I like red wine vinegar for general eating, rice vinegar to pair with stir-fry or noodles, and lime for Mexican-inspired bowls or tacos), and a pinch of salt. Let rest for 10 to 15 minutes to allow the dressing to penetrate and soften the cabbage.

Quick-Pickled Cabbage or Onion

Sour quick-pickled veggies are a great addition to not only bowls but tacos, sandwiches, and salads as well. Thinly slice white or red onion, or red or green cabbage—enough to fit in a sealable jar. Red onions and red cabbage make a particularly pretty pink quick pickle. Place in a jar submerged in equal parts water and vinegar—I like to use apple cider or regular white vinegar, or a combo. This will be ready to serve after about 30 minutes, or store in the fridge for a couple of weeks.

Cilantro-Lime Cream

Sauces

Sauces are the secret weapon in the fight against bland, boring bowls. Plain rice, chickpeas, and kale are utterly transformed by the addition of Tahini-Lemon Sauce. And nothing says "sweater weather" more than potatoes smothered in my favourite Nearly Instant Gravy. All sauces can be made in advance and stored in an airtight container in the fridge for up to 5 days. They make enough for 4 to 8 servings.

Tahini-Lemon Sauce

This creamy, lemony sauce is one of my long-time favourites. Not only is it delicious and nutritious, it is also fast to make and doesn't require a blender. You can doctor up this tahini-lemon sauce by adding all kinds of other ingredients—miso, soy sauce, minced garlic, garlic powder—but for the most part, I like to keep it simple. Add to a jar or bowl: ⅓ cup (80 mL) tahini, the juice of 1 lemon, 3 Tbsp (45 mL) water, and a pinch of salt. Shake or whisk until smooth. If needed, add water 1 Tbsp (15 mL) at a time to thin it out. It may need to be thinned with additional water after refrigeration.

Tip

Some tahinis can be bitter. Shop around until you find a brand that you like. My favourite is by Arz Fine Foods, which has a nice pourable consistency, but there are many wonderful options.

Cilantro-Lime Cream

Tangy, creamy, and full of cilantro, this sauce is good not only on bowls but also on tacos and nachos. We're blending cashews here, so if you know your blender will struggle to get the nuts fully smooth, start by first soaking them in water for 30 minutes. Then, in a blender, blend ½ cup (125 mL) cashews, ⅓ cup (80 mL) water, juice of 1 lime, 1 clove garlic, ½ cup (125 mL) gently packed cilantro (tough stems removed), and ½ tsp (2 mL) salt until smooth. Add additional water if needed to attain your desired consistency. If the sauce separates when stored in the fridge, shake or whisk before use.

Citrus-Hemp Sauce

This mild, creamy sauce is versatile and kid-friendly. The garlic cuts the grassiness of the hemp, and the orange juice adds a hint of sweetness to soften the lemon. In a blender, blend ½ cup (125 mL) hemp seeds, ⅓ cup (80 mL) orange juice, juice of 1 lemon, 1 to 2 cloves garlic, and ½ tsp (2 mL) salt on high until smooth. If the sauce separates when stored in the fridge, shake or whisk before use.

Super Speedy Salsa

Jazz up your rice and beans with salsa made in a food processor, no dicing required. Start by processing 1 to 2 cloves garlic until minced. Then add 3 Roma tomatoes cut into chunks—or sub about 2 heaping cups (550 mL) of any other type of cut tomato, or 1 (14 oz/398 mL) can diced tomatoes; ½ small white or red onion cut into chunks (about 1 heaping cup/275 mL); a small handful of cilantro, tough stems removed (about ½ cup/125 mL, packed); and salt to taste. Pulse until evenly chopped with some texture remaining. Optionally, add the juice of ½ lime.

Nearly Instant Gravy

This weeknight-friendly gravy requires no chopping, just a few ingredients, and best of all, no foresight! Drown your potato-based bowls in it. In a room-temperature medium saucepan, combine 3 Tbsp (45 mL) chickpea flour with 2 Tbsp (30 mL) extra virgin olive oil—you'll get a viscous yellow mixture. Set over medium heat and cook the mixture by allowing it to gently bubble and toast for a minute. Now stream in 1½ cups (375 mL) water, whisking constantly. Whisk in 2 Tbsp (30 mL) soy sauce, 1 tsp (5 mL) onion powder, 1 tsp (5 mL) garlic powder, and ½ tsp (2 mL) ground sage or poultry seasoning. Simmer for a few minutes, whisking often, to thicken the gravy and combine the flavours. To reheat, whisk in a saucepan over medium heat, adding water 1 Tbsp (15 mL) at a time as needed to thin it out.

Fresh Herb Purée

Made with plenty of fresh herbs, this green condiment brightens up bowls and sandwiches. I also love it for flavouring polenta. To prepare the herbs, rinse them and chop off the tough stems. The water that clings to the herbs after rinsing will contribute moisture to the purée, so don't worry about vigorously drying them. This will seem like a lot of herbs, but they reduce an astonishing amount. In a food processor, process 1 to 2 cloves garlic to chop it. Then add 1 bunch cilantro, 1 bunch parsley, 1 heaping Tbsp (20 mL) light-coloured miso, 1 Tbsp (15 mL) red wine vinegar, and 3 Tbsp (45 mL) extra virgin olive oil, and process until puréed.

Tip

Miso comes in several types, which can be a bit overwhelming when trying to choose which to buy. Generally, the lighter (white or yellow) varieties have a milder flavour and are what I use for vegan-cooking umami boosts. I like the white (aka "white type") miso by Hikari Miso.

Nearly Instant Gravy

Toppings

Toppings are an opportunity to add extra texture, flavour, and nutrition, and can include nuts or seeds (especially toasted, yum!), dried fruits or veg, pickled or brined components, fresh herbs, and finishing salts. This is the component that can really make a dish seem beautiful and even a little fancy, even though it only takes a moment.

To toast nuts or seeds, first chop any larger nuts. Then simply cook in a dry pan over medium heat until brown, shaking often, about 5 minutes. Alternatively, if you have the oven on at a lowish heat (like 350°F/175°C or lower), toast the nuts or seeds on a baking sheet, shaking after about 5 minutes—they should be crisp and brown in 8 to 10 minutes.

Nuts

- Almonds (chopped or slivered)
- Cashews
- Hazelnuts
- Macadamia nuts
- Pecans
- Pine nuts
- Pistachios
- Walnuts

Seeds

- Hemp seeds
- Pumpkin seeds
- Sesame seeds
- Sunflower seeds

Dried Fruits and Veg

- Dates
- Dried cranberries
- Raisins
- Sun-dried tomatoes

Pickled or Brined Things

- Capers
- Dill pickles
- Kimchi
- Olives
- Sauerkraut

Fresh Herbs

- Basil
- Chives
- Cilantro
- Dill
- Mint
- Parsley

Spices and Dried Herbs

- Chili flakes
- Dried basil
- Dried dill
- Dried mint
- Dried tarragon
- Nigella seeds
- Paprika (sweet or smoked)
- Sumac

Polenta, Lemon-Garlic Cannellini Beans (page 138), chopped lettuce and kale, Fresh Herb Purée (page 156), toasted sunflower seeds

Putting It All Together:
Some of My Favourite Bowls

You can mix and match the recipes and suggestions in this chapter to create your own bowls. Here are a few of my favourite combinations. They all contain a variety of textures, have complementary flavours, and are practical even on weeknights. You'll see they're organized by legume, which is really at the heart of a bowl, in my opinion.

LEGUME	GRAIN/STARCH	VEGGIE	SAUCE	TOPPING
Black beans, drained and rinsed	Quinoa	Seared Peppers and Onions (page 148)	Cilantro-Lime Cream (page 155)	Thinly sliced green onion
Saucy Simple Mexican-Inspired Black Beans (page 136)	Roasted sweet potatoes (cubed or halved)	Lettuce tossed with extra virgin olive oil; freshly squeezed lime juice	Super Speedy Salsa (page 155)	Smoked paprika
Cannellini beans, drained and rinsed	Brown rice	Roasted Root Veggies (page 147)	Nearly Instant Gravy (page 156)	Chopped fresh parsley
Cannellini beans, drained and rinsed	Polenta	Blistered Cherry Tomatoes with Garlic and Basil (page 151)		Chopped toasted walnuts
Cannellini beans, drained and rinsed	Steamed new potatoes	Garlic-Wilted Spring Greens (page 147)	Citrus-Hemp Sauce (page 155)	Sauerkraut
Lemon-Garlic Cannellini Beans (page 138)	Polenta	Chopped leafy greens (like kale or lettuce)	Fresh Herb Purée (page 156)	Sunflower seeds
Lemon-Garlic Cannellini Beans (page 138)	Brown rice	Lemony Arugula and Herbs (page 148)		Capers; chopped toasted almonds
Chickpeas, drained and rinsed	Roasted sweet potatoes (cubed or halved)	Roasted Asparagus (page 148); Blistered Cherry Tomatoes with Garlic and Basil (page 151)	Tahini-Lemon Sauce (page 155)	Chopped fresh basil
Five-Minute Paprika-Spiked Chickpeas and Greens (page 140)	Mashed potatoes		Fresh Herb Purée (page 156)	Hemp seeds

chart continues

LEGUME	GRAIN/STARCH	VEGGIE	SAUCE	TOPPING
Five-Minute Paprika-Spiked Chickpeas and Greens (page 140)	Toasted sourdough or bread	Grated Carrot Salad (page 151)		Chopped fresh parsley
Sheet Pan Chickpeas and Cauliflower (page 145)	Quinoa	Chopped lettuce	Drizzle of extra virgin olive oil; freshly squeezed lemon juice	Kalamata olives
Sheet Pan Chickpeas and Cauliflower (page 145)	Roasted potatoes (cubed)	Chopped leafy greens (like kale or lettuce)	Tahini-Lemon Sauce (page 155)	Sumac
Oil-Free Hummus (page 214)	Brown rice	Steamed or roasted cauliflower; chopped cucumber	Tahini-Lemon Sauce (page 155)	Toasted sesame seeds
Steamed edamame	Brown rice	Shredded carrots; thinly sliced cucumber	Soy sauce; sesame oil	Toasted sesame seeds; thinly sliced toasted nori sheets
Lentils in Garlicky Red Wine Vinaigrette (page 139)	Polenta	Avocado-Rubbed Kale (page 151)		Hemp seeds
Lentils in Garlicky Red Wine Vinaigrette (page 139)	Roasted sweet potatoes (cubed or halved)	Blackened Broccoli (page 148)	Freshly squeezed lemon juice	Thinly sliced green onion
Saucy Simple Mexican-Inspired Pinto Beans (page 136)	Brown rice	Cabbage Slaw (page 151)		Toasted pumpkin seeds
Savoury Pan-Crisped Tofu Cubes (page 142)	Mashed potatoes	Steamed broccoli	Nearly Instant Gravy (page 156)	Hemp seeds
Savoury Pan-Crisped Tofu Cubes (page 142)	Soba noodles	Blackened Broccoli (page 148)	Soy sauce; sesame oil (on the noodles)	Toasted sesame seeds; thinly sliced green onion
White Bean Purée (page 215)	Quinoa	Lemony Arugula and Herbs (page 148)		Chopped dates; chopped almonds

Mashed potatoes, Savoury Pan-Crisped Tofu Cubes (page 142),
steamed broccoli, Nearly Instant Gravy (page 156)

One-Pot Wednesday

Stews and soups represent one of the oldest styles of cooking and eating. For many thousands of years, humans around the globe have been simmering pots of grains, tubers, meats, and vegetables over fires and stoves, making the ingredients of their environment delicious and digestible.

Do you know the story of stone soup? As the fable goes, food is scarce but the villagers all add a little something to a communal soup pot—one family adds a carrot, another a potato, another some beans, and so on. Eventually, a delicious pot of soup is created, so much more than the sum of its parts. The story is supposed to teach the value of sharing, but I think it also teaches the value of soup. You can add this and that, simmer it together, and you get a delicious meal.

On Wednesdays, in the middle of our week, I make an easy, cozy pot of soup or stew. My kids absolutely love Corn Soup with Sneaky Red Lentils (page 172). My personal favourite is Black Bean and Tomato Soup with Toasted Fennel Seed (page 179). I make The Easiest Curried Red Lentils (page 181) at least twice a month, because everyone in my family eats them happily, and it's not only truly easy to make but also pantry-friendly, for those days you're not as prepared.

Do cook beans from dried for soups, if you have it in you—see page 133 for how. The starchy water you are left with after the beans are cooked is ideal for adding body and flavour to soups. It's fine to use canned beans, though, and I do this sometimes myself when I don't have cooked beans prepared. I suggest you either rinse canned beans and then add additional water or stock, or seek out canned beans that don't contain preservatives (like disodium EDTA or calcium chloride). These preservative-free cans can be used in their entirety, beans and their cooking liquid, and they're delicious in soups.

Let's canvas a few of the ways soups and stews are amazing: they require only one pot (or two, if you're making rice), so we don't have to manage separate components, and clean-up is a relative breeze. They're nutritious and digestible; I always feel good with a belly full of soup. It's easy to add beans and lentils—which many of us try to eat more of—to these dishes. They scale up to feed guests or for intentional leftovers. Maybe best of all, soups and stews only get better in the fridge! I can't think of another meal that sits there overnight getting more delicious with absolutely no input from me.

How to Make Soup: A Weeknight Guide

Soup has to be up there as one of the most versatile meals one can learn how to cook. Recipes are useful when we're starting out as cooks, so that we can understand how soups are made. They're also a great way to get new soup ideas, especially when we feel stuck in a rut. But one of my favourite things about soup is that it can be made from just about any veggies, grains, starches, legumes, herbs, and spices we like *without* a recipe. Here are the principles that I mentally run through when I freestyle a pot of soup.

Chop some onion and garlic

Onion and garlic are key for providing a boost of flavour. I find that, with these as my base, I can get away with using water rather than stock, keeping things simpler and more economical. Onions and garlic match with virtually any cuisine—from Indian to French to Mexican—so you can be confident that starting with sautéed onion and garlic is foolproof.

Choose your fat (s)

There are two general opportunities to add fat to your soup: at the beginning, to sauté your first few ingredients, or later, to add dimension and mouthfeel. Extra virgin olive oil is my stove-side all-purpose oil, and it's nearly always what I reach for to gently sauté onions and garlic in.

Adding a can of full-fat coconut milk is a sure way to make soup irresistible—it works well with other tropical flavours, as in coconut curries and Thai-inspired soups. A spoonful of tahini mixed in at the end is an easy way to add richness to Mediterranean-inspired soups. And a bit of cashew cream (simply blend together equal parts cashews and water) is a great swap for dairy-based cream.

Choose your veggies

The beauty of making soup is that you can use practically any veggies that are good cooked. I generally stick with one to three kinds. Chop them into bite-sized pieces and add them working backwards, starting with those that take the longest to cook and working up to those that take the shortest time. Root veggies like potatoes and carrots take the longest, about 15 minutes when chopped—or even longer to get them falling-apart tender. Most veggies, from peppers to beans to cauliflower, are somewhere in the middle, taking 5 to 10 minutes. Veggies boil much faster in water than they do in some kind of starchy broth, where the boiling point is lower. Leafy greens are best added near the end, in the last few minutes of cooking. When in doubt, consider whether you'd rather something be overcooked or undercooked—I'd rather have overcooked carrots and undercooked kale, for example—and govern yourself accordingly.

Consider including a starch

If you include anything starchy—potatoes, beans, lentils, flour, or pasta—some of the starch will infuse the broth with a wonderful creaminess:

- **Potatoes:** If you cook cubed potatoes for 15 to 20 minutes, they'll start to disintegrate into the soup, which is lovely. Potato soup is a classic for a reason.
- **Beans:** Adding a few scoops (or cans) of beans, along with their cooking liquid, is always a good idea. Beans are delicious in many forms, but I believe they especially shine in soups, where they absorb flavour and, in turn, impart creaminess.
- **Lentils:** I always have lentils in my pantry, since they require zero foresight to use. Split lentils—such as red—by design break down into soup to make it creamy and thickened, and they cook especially quickly.
- **Flour:** You can add 2 to 3 Tbsp (30 to 45 mL) flour to brown along with your softened onion before whisking in liquid to help thicken the broth. I like using chickpea flour for this purpose.
- **Pasta:** In a minestrone-inspired soup, a few handfuls of any kind of pasta can be delicious and make your soup extra hearty. I like to keep small, quick-cooking pasta shapes on hand for tossing directly into pots of soup. If you prefer, you can first cook the pasta al dente, to cut down on cooking time once added to the soup or if you want to minimize the starch added.

Choose your liquid

Homemade stock is easy enough to make, but it does require a little effort: you need to save scraps, simmer the stock, then store it either in the fridge (remembering to use it before it goes bad) or in the freezer (remembering to thaw it before you actually need it). All this for a nice, but unnecessary, component can feel like a bridge too far sometimes. Commercial stocks are also an option, but the aseptic containers can feel wasteful, while the concentrates tend to have ingredients lists that can be a little off-putting.

For these reasons, I mostly use water as the base of soups, and it's absolutely fine. There's plenty of flavour to be found in onions, garlic, and any other veggies and seasonings that are part of the soup. If I'm including home-cooked beans in my soup, I generally use the creamy, starchy, flavourful water they were cooked in, too. What I'm saying is, use whatever works for you, but don't be afraid of using water.

Choose your seasonings

I used to think bay leaves were a hoax and always left them out of recipes. Now I appreciate the subtle complexity they add to simmered dishes, and I almost always add a few to my soups. If you're a bay leaf skeptic, like I was, I can only ask you to trust that they're worth using. They're probably not something that you'll taste, exactly, but they will add a dimension that you'll enjoy. Just don't forget to remove before serving or blending.

We all have our preferred herbs and spices. I'm partial to lots of paprika, pungent garlic powder, citrusy ground coriander, and whole toasted fennel seeds. There are also natural flavour pairings—cumin and black bean, oregano and tomato, cinnamon and sweet potato. There is no surer way to learn what spices you like in your soup than to smell the spices, cook with them, and reflect on how well you like the taste. Playing around with dried herbs and spices is an easy way to introduce variety into our cooking year-round.

Add dried herbs and spices after the oil, onion, and garlic to allow their aroma compounds to toast a little and infuse the cooking oil so they disperse throughout the soup. Any fresh herbs are probably best stirred in at the end of cooking or simply sprinkled on top of your bowl of soup.

To blend or not to blend?

When it comes to the consistency of your soup, you have basically three choices. You can blend your soup, leave your soup chunky, or blend some of your soup and pour it back into the pot for a cream soup with texture. I like some texture in my soup, but I find kids are more likely to enjoy cream soup. Sometimes, I'll blend only theirs and leave the rest as is for Arden and me to enjoy. Most soups are good any of these ways, meaning that family members can eat the same soup but according to their preference.

Corn Soup with Sneaky Red Lentils

Serves 6

One of the first soups I ever loved was chowder, which really spoke to my childhood need to eat creamy foods as often as possible. Although I've branched out in my food tastes, I continue to adore this lighter-but-still-rich corn soup. It's an especially good one to feed lentil skeptics; the lentils disintegrate, leaving a creamy soup with pops of sweet corn. This is a major kid favourite at my place.

1. Heat a large pot over medium heat. Add the oil, onion, and a pinch of salt and sauté until the onion is soft and translucent.

2. Add the garlic and bay leaves and sauté for another minute.

3. Add the potato, lentils, and water or stock. Season with salt and pepper. Simmer, covered, for 10 minutes. Then add the corn and simmer for another 10 minutes, or until the lentils have disintegrated. Remove the bay leaves.

4. Transfer 2 cups (500 mL) of the soup to a blender, along with the cashews, if using. Blend until very smooth, then return the puréed soup to the pot, stirring to combine.

5. Refrigerate any leftovers in an airtight container for 4 to 5 days. Avoid freezing this soup, since it contains potato.

2 to 3 tsp (10 to 15 mL) extra virgin olive oil

1 medium onion, diced

4 cloves garlic, minced

2 bay leaves

1 lb (454 g) yellow or red potatoes, scrubbed and cut into ¾-inch (2 cm) chunks (about 3 heaping cups/825 mL) chopped)

1½ cups (375 mL) red lentils, rinsed

8 cups water or stock

Salt and pepper

3 cups (750 mL) frozen corn kernels

½ cup (125 mL) cashews (optional; see Tip)

Tip

If you don't want to use cashews, you can easily skip them—I sometimes leave them out for a lighter summer soup. I don't soak the cashews, because I use a high-speed blender and because I find that blending them with the hot soup softens them anyway. If your blender struggles to get cashews smooth, you have three options:

1. Add the cashews to the pot along with the water or stock to boil. They will soften along with the rest of the soup.

2. Soak the cashews for at least 30 minutes ahead of time, then use as directed in step 4.

3. Blend the soup for a long time—I'm talking 5 minutes or so. In all my years of cooking in other people's homes and in vacation rental kitchens, I've never met a blender that couldn't get raw cashews smooth when given enough time. Just be sure to pause the blender if it starts to feel hot to avoid blowing out the motor.

Creamy Potato White Bean Soup

Serves 8

Potatoes make an excellent base for soup—they sort of melt into the broth, making it lovely and creamy. My kids especially like this potato soup blended smooth into cream-of-potato soup; Arden and I leave ours unblended, which is creamy enough but still has some texture. This recipe makes a large pot of soup, but since potato soup doesn't freeze well, halve it if you're not cooking for a crowd or you don't want leftovers (though soup is always better the next day!).

1. Heat a large pot over medium heat. Add the oil, then the onion and carrot, along with a pinch of salt. Sauté until the onion is soft and translucent.

2. Add the garlic and sauté for another minute. Then add the paprika and bay leaves to toast. Stir until they start to stick, about 1 minute.

3. Add the potatoes, beans with their cooking liquid, and water or stock. Season with salt and pepper. Simmer, covered, for 15 minutes, or until the potatoes are very soft and to your liking.

4. Allow the soup to sit off the heat, uncovered, for a further 10 minutes, if you can, to allow the flavours to develop and the soup to thicken. Remove the bay leaves.

5. If blending, ladle the soup into a blender, filling it no more than two-thirds full. Blend on medium speed until very smooth, allowing the steam to escape so it doesn't build up and blow the lid off your blender. Repeat with additional batches if necessary.

6. Serve with a drizzle of olive oil and vinegar for those who like it. Refrigerate any leftovers in an airtight container for 4 to 5 days. The only downside to potato soup is that it doesn't freeze well, so enjoy this one now.

2 to 3 tsp (10 to 15 mL) extra virgin olive oil, plus more for serving

1 medium onion, diced

1 cup (250 mL) diced carrot

4 cloves garlic, minced

1 Tbsp (15 mL) sweet paprika

3 bay leaves

2 lb (900 g) yellow potatoes, scrubbed and chopped into ¾-inch (2 cm) chunks (about 6 cups/1.5 L chopped)

4 cups (1 L) cooked cannellini (white kidney) beans, including their cooking liquid (or sub 1⅓ cups/330 mL water or stock)

5 cups (1.25 L) water or stock

Salt and pepper

Apple cider or red wine vinegar, for serving (optional)

Variations

For picky eaters: If you're cooking for picky eaters who won't like the orange colour of this soup, peel the potatoes and omit the carrots and paprika—you'll end up with a white soup.

Herb and spice options: Instead of paprika, add 1½ tsp (7 mL) poultry seasoning or herbes de Provence. For a brighter, more citrusy soup, instead of paprika use 1½ tsp (7 mL) ground coriander, and finish with a squeeze of lemon juice.

Make it a meal

I like to ladle my soup into a big bowl of finely chopped greens, like kale or arugula. The hot soup wilts the greens, and I love the texture and contrast this provides. My kids love buttered toast cut into squares to dunk into theirs.

Lemony Chickpea and Rice Soup

Serves 6

Some form of lemony legume-and-rice soup has been in Arden's and my meal rotation for almost as many years as we've been cooking together—through different kitchens and life stages, it has been a constant. I make it with either brown jasmine rice or a multigrain rice blend, both of which cook in about 25 minutes. If you use a rice with a longer cooking time, hold off on adding the chickpeas until the last 20 or 25 minutes so they don't get too soft (unless you like them that way).

1. Heat a large pot over medium heat. Add the oil, onion, and a pinch of salt and sauté the onion until soft and translucent.

2. Add the garlic and stir, giving the garlic a 30-second head start on the spices.

3. Stir in the coriander, cumin, and bay leaves and toast for 1 minute.

4. Add the chickpeas and their cooking liquid, rice, and water or stock. Season with salt and pepper. Cover and bring to a boil, then reduce to a simmer. Simmer, covered and stirring occasionally, until the rice is tender, about 25 minutes.

5. Add the lemon zest and juice and taste for flavour, adjusting seasonings as needed.

6. Refrigerate any leftovers in an airtight container for 4 to 5 days. Grains in soup don't retain a great texture when frozen then thawed, so I recommend enjoying this soup while fresh.

2 to 3 tsp (10 to 15 mL) extra virgin olive oil

1 medium onion, diced

4 cloves garlic, minced

2 tsp (10 mL) ground coriander

1½ tsp (7 mL) cumin

2 bay leaves

3 cups (750 mL) cooked chickpeas, including their cooking liquid (or sub 1 cup/250 mL water or stock)

1 cup (250 mL) brown jasmine rice or multigrain rice blend

5 cups (1.25 L) water or stock

Salt and pepper

Zest and juice of 1½ lemons

French Lentil and Mushroom Soup with Miso and Rosemary

French lentils and rosemary work so well together, both being earthy and peppery and tasting like autumn. Umami-rich miso and mushrooms add depth and heartiness that belie the simple ingredients list. This soup pairs nicely with a roaring fire.

1. Heat a large pot over medium heat. Add the oil, onion, mushrooms, and a pinch of salt and sauté until soft.

2. Stir in the garlic and rosemary and cook another 30 seconds or so, until fragrant and well combined.

3. Add the lentils and 7 cups (1.75 L) water or stock. Bring to a boil, then simmer, covered, for 20 to 25 minutes, until the lentils are tender (sample a few of them to be sure). Add up to an additional 1 cup (250 mL) water or stock if you prefer a brothier soup. Remove the rosemary sprigs.

4. Ladle out about ½ cup (125 mL) of broth into a bowl and dissolve the miso into it. Add to the pot and stir to combine.

5. Season generously with pepper, and taste for salt—it may not need it because of the miso.

6. Refrigerate any leftovers in an airtight container for 4 to 5 days. Reheat gently, cooking until the soup is steaming; avoid boiling, as that will kill the beneficial microorganisms in the miso.

2 to 3 tsp (10 to 15 mL) extra virgin olive oil

1 medium onion, diced

8 oz (225 g) cremini mushrooms, sliced

4 cloves garlic, minced

3 (6-inch/16 cm) sprigs fresh rosemary (or sub 1 Tbsp/15 mL dried)

1½ cups (375 mL) French lentils

7 to 8 cups (1.75 to 2 L) water or stock

3 Tbsp (45 mL) miso, any type (I use white, but a darker one would work too)

Salt and pepper

Make it a meal

This lentil soup is so good with fresh bread to dunk into it. I also like it served on fresh polenta. Add a crisp green salad dressed with Everyday Vinaigrette (page 76) on the side.

Variation

With greens: Add a few handfuls of finely chopped kale, or your favourite green, at the end of cooking just to wilt—to get your greens in and provide an additional layer of texture.

Black Bean and Tomato Soup with Toasted Fennel Seed

Serves 4

I take a page from Indian cooking techniques and toast whole fennel seeds in a little oil before adding the onion to sauté. This simple step adds a world of flavour. If I had to choose a favourite soup, this would probably be it; the combination of browned onion, fragrant fennel, tangy tomatoes, and hearty black beans is a match made in heaven.

1. Heat a large pot over medium heat. Add the oil and fennel seeds. Sauté until the seeds turn brown.

2. Add the onion and a pinch of salt, stirring constantly until the onion comes up to temperature, to prevent them from sticking to the pan. Cook until the onion is soft and translucent.

3. Add the garlic, oregano, and bay leaves and sauté until toasty and fragrant, about 30 seconds.

4. Add the tomatoes, beans, and 1½ cups (375 mL) water or stock. Season with salt and pepper.

5. Bring to a simmer and cook partially covered for at least 10 minutes to combine and deepen flavours. Add an additional ½ cup (125 mL) water or stock if the soup seems too thick for your liking.

6. Remove from the heat and remove the bay leaves. Taste and adjust for salt and pepper. Serve with a drizzle of olive oil, if you'd like.

7. Refrigerate any leftovers in an airtight container for up to 5 days, or freeze for up to 3 months.

2 to 3 tsp (10 to 15 mL) extra virgin olive oil, plus more for serving

1½ tsp (7 mL) fennel seeds

1 medium onion, diced

4 cloves garlic, minced

1 tsp (5 mL) dried oregano

2 bay leaves

1 (28 oz/796 mL) can tomatoes—crushed, diced, or whole peeled (squished) (see Tip)

2 cups (500 mL) cooked black beans, including their cooking liquid (or sub ⅔ cup/160 mL water or stock)

1½ to 2 cups (375 to 500 mL) water or stock

Salt and pepper

Tip

Any type of canned tomato works here, and I use whatever I have. Crushed tomatoes make a smoother soup. Diced tomatoes add a little more texture. If I had to pick a favourite, it would be whole peeled: add them to the pot one by one, squishing them up in your clean hand as you do, before pouring in any remaining juice from the can. This creates a varied, slurpable texture, one I find absolutely delicious. Plus, squishing tomatoes in your hand is just fun.

recipe continues

Make it a meal

Serve with a vinaigrette-dressed green salad, or stir some finely chopped greens right into the soup at the end of cooking to wilt. Pair it with a grain or starch, such as bread or polenta. I like to drop my cooked polenta right on top of my tomato soup, kind of like a cousin of shakshuka.

Variations

Cream of Tomato Soup: Scoop one to two ladlefuls of the soup into a blender and blend until very smooth. Optionally, add a ⅓ cup (80 mL) cashews or hemp seeds and ⅓ cup (80 mL) water before blending. This is how my kids like it, because it's smooth and very creamy.

With white beans: Half the time I make this soup with white beans, which works equally well. My favourite are creamy cannellini beans, which are also known as white kidney beans.

With quinoa: Sometimes I add 1 cup (250 mL) uncooked quinoa, along with an additional 2 cups (500 mL) water or stock, and cook the soup for a total of 15 minutes. This adds substance and makes the soup a complete meal.

Smoky Black Bean and Tomato Soup with Toasted Cumin Seed: Swap the fennel seeds for cumin seeds. Add 1 tsp (5 mL) smoked paprika along with the oregano.

The Easiest Curried Red Lentils

Serves 4 to 6

Red lentils are one of my favourite legumes: they cook quickly—in about 20 minutes as long as there's nothing acidic added—and they don't need to be soaked. As lentils that have been split in half, much like split peas, they fall apart when cooked, and make a thick soup or stew that I find incredibly satisfying. They have a fairly neutral flavour, so they can take on whatever spices and aromatics you cook them with. This lentil dish, inspired by Indian dal, involves no chopping, and it's what I often make at the end of a long day when I. Just. Cannot.

Stovetop

1. Heat a large pot over medium heat. Add the oil, then the turmeric, cumin, and coriander. Toast until fragrant—this will take only a matter of seconds, as ground spices toast quickly.

2. Add the lentils, water, garlic powder, and salt, and season with black pepper. Mix together.

3. Cover and bring to a boil, then reduce to a simmer. Simmer, covered and stirring occasionally, for 20 minutes, or until the lentils have fallen apart and are very soft.

Pressure Cooker

1. Set your pressure cooker to sauté. Add the oil, turmeric, cumin, and coriander. Toast until fragrant—this will take only a matter of seconds, as ground spices toast quickly.

2. Add the lentils, water, garlic powder, and salt, and season with black pepper. Mix together.

3. Lock the lid and set to 6 minutes at high pressure. It's okay to quick release the pressure, since you can't harm the texture, or to allow it to come down naturally until you're ready to eat. Give the lentils a vigorous stir to fully incorporate everything.

For Both

4. If the stew is too thick, add water 1 Tbsp (15 mL) at a time to thin it out to your liking. To serve, garnish with cilantro and a squeeze of lime, if desired.

5. Refrigerate any leftovers in an airtight container for up to 5 days, or freeze for up to 3 months. These lentils thicken significantly in the fridge; to reheat leftovers, whisk in 3 to 4 Tbsp (45 to 60 mL) water and an additional big pinch of salt and heat through.

1½ Tbsp (22 mL) extra virgin olive oil

1 tsp (5 mL) turmeric

2 tsp (10 mL) ground cumin

2 tsp (10 mL) ground coriander

2 cups (500 mL) red lentils, rinsed

5 cups (1.25 L) water

1½ tsp (7 mL) garlic powder

1½ tsp (7 mL) salt

Black pepper

Fresh cilantro and lime, for serving (optional)

recipe continues

Make it a meal

I like this red lentil stew ladled on top of a bit of brown rice or quinoa and a big bed of greens, like kale or arugula. Cabbage Slaw (page 151) is also good on the side, providing contrasting texture and tangy flavour. To keep it simple, pair with toast. Top with fresh cilantro, more fresh cracked pepper, and a squeeze of lemon or lime juice. I really like it with some mango pickle condiment on the side.

Variations

With onions, garlic, ginger, and tomato: You can, of course, add the customary aromatics here. Dice 1 onion, mince 4 cloves of garlic and a thumb of ginger, and chop 1 to 2 tomatoes. Sauté the onion in a little oil until soft; add the garlic and ginger and cook for a minute until fragrant; add the turmeric, cumin, and coriander from the recipe and toast for another minute, then add the tomato and simmer vigorously until the liquid is reduced slightly. Proceed with step 2, but don't add any garlic powder.

Coconut Curried Red Lentils: Replace 1½ cups (375 mL) of the water with 1 (14 oz/398 mL) can of full-fat coconut milk for a richer and more filling end product.

Using spice blends: Replace the spices with your favourite curry powder, and add a pinch of garam masala for even more warmth.

Chocolate Chili
with Toasted Cumin Seed

Serves 6 to 8

As soon as cool weather hits in the fall, I automatically make a warming, hearty pot of chili. It heralds the change in seasons to me as much as scarves and mittens do. Cocoa powder is bitter and complex, and it works very well in savoury cooking; think of Mexican mole sauce. The recipe as written retains some crisp texture in the bell pepper—sauté it along with the onion instead if you like it meltingly soft.

1. Heat a large pot over medium heat. Add the oil and then the cumin seeds, stirring to coat. The cumin seeds will start to dance a little, become fragrant, and turn a darker shade of brown in about 30 seconds. Add the onion and a pinch of salt and sauté until the onion is soft and translucent.

2. Add the garlic, paprika, and oregano. Stir to combine and toast until fragrant and sticking to the pan, about 30 seconds.

3. Add the tomatoes and stir well, deglazing the pan by scraping up any stuck browned bits from the bottom with a wooden spoon. Then add the kidney beans, black beans, lentils, bell pepper, water or stock, and cocoa powder. Season with salt and pepper.

4. Simmer, partially covered and stirring occasionally, until the tomatoes are soft, the bell pepper is just tender, and all is well combined, about 10 minutes. Taste and adjust the salt and pepper.

5. Refrigerate any leftovers in an airtight container for up to 5 days, or freeze for up to 6 months.

2 to 3 tsp (10 to 15 mL) extra virgin olive oil

1½ tsp (7 mL) cumin seeds

1 medium onion, diced

4 cloves garlic, minced

1½ Tbsp (22 mL) sweet paprika

1½ tsp (7 mL) dried oregano

3 cups (750 mL) fresh or 1 (28 oz/796 mL) can diced tomatoes

2 cups (500 mL) cooked kidney beans, drained and rinsed

2 cups (500 mL) cooked black beans, drained and rinsed

2 cups (500 mL) cooked brown or green lentils, drained and rinsed

1 medium green bell pepper, diced

1 cup (250 mL) water or stock

2 Tbsp (30 mL) cocoa powder

Salt and pepper

Variation

With red lentils: I love to add red lentils too, because they break down into the sauce to make for an extra thick, hearty chili. It increases the cooking time, however, especially because lentils take longer to cook in the presence of acidity (the tomatoes). When you have a little extra time, add ½ cup (125 mL) rinsed red lentils and an additional 1 cup (250 mL) water or stock along with the beans and brown or green lentils. Instead of simmering for only 10 minutes, you'll need to simmer for 25 to 30 minutes, or until the red lentils are soft.

Make it a meal

Serve the chili scooped onto baked potatoes or polenta, with bread, or simply on its own. A crisp green salad or tangy slaw on the side will add texture, a nicely contrasting sour flavour, and a dose of veggies. Top it with cool, creamy avocado, if you have some.

Chickpea Cauliflower Curry

Serves 4 to 6

One of the easiest ways to double the deliciousness factor of a pot of soup or stew is to add coconut milk. It adds an irresistible creamy body, and here it works especially well with the sour notes from the tomatoes and lime. (I do sometimes skip the tomatoes, if I don't have them; the lime provides enough acidity on its own.) This curry comes together super fast because we're starting with cooked legumes. It's a family favourite.

1. Heat a large pot over medium heat. Add the oil and then the cumin seeds, stirring to coat. The cumin seeds will start to dance a little, become fragrant, and turn a darker shade of brown in about 30 seconds. Add the onion and a pinch of salt and sauté until the onion is soft and translucent.

2. Add the garlic and sauté until fragrant, about 30 seconds. Stir in the coriander and turmeric and toast for 1 minute, until sticking to the pan.

3. Add the tomatoes and stir well, deglazing the pan by scraping up any stuck browned bits from the bottom with a wooden spoon. Increase the heat to medium-high. Simmer the mixture until the tomatoes start to break apart, about 2 minutes.

4. Add the chickpeas, cauliflower, coconut milk, and water. Season with salt and pepper. Stir together and bring to a simmer.

5. Cover and reduce the heat just to maintain a gentle simmer. Simmer the curry until the cauliflower is fork-tender to your liking, 10 to 15 minutes.

6. Turn off the heat and stir in the lime juice. Taste and adjust the seasonings.

2 to 3 tsp (10 to 15 mL) extra virgin olive oil

2 tsp (10 mL) cumin seeds (for ground, see Tip)

1 medium onion, diced

4 cloves garlic, minced

1 Tbsp (15 mL) ground coriander

1 tsp (5 mL) turmeric

1½ cups (375 mL) fresh or 1 (14 oz/398 mL) can diced tomatoes (optional)

4 cups (1 L) cooked chickpeas, drained and rinsed

1 medium head cauliflower, cut into bite-sized florets

1 (14 oz/398 mL) can full-fat coconut milk

½ cup (125 mL) water

Salt and pepper

Juice of 1 lime

Make it a meal

I like my cauliflower curry scooped over a bed of brown jasmine rice and chopped hearty greens, like kale or spinach, which just wilt under the heat of the curry. A big handful of cilantro on top is nice, too. Or try it ladled onto baked russet or sweet potatoes. We usually keep a jar of mango pickle in the fridge, for the adults to add some heat and sourness on the side. You'll find mango pickle in the Indian section of your supermarket.

Tip

To use ground instead of whole cumin, you can simply add the ground cumin along with the other ground spices in step 2. Start by sautéing the onion until soft. Add the garlic, then the coriander, turmeric, and 2 tsp (10 mL) ground cumin and proceed with the recipe.

Stir-Fry Thursday

By Thursday, I've been cooking all week, in addition to juggling the many other things that make family life so beautifully chaotic. The first of the weekend vibes are in the air. This is when feelings of "dinner needs to be cooked . . . *again*?!" may start to creep in. An easy stir-fry is just what I need to breathe a little sigh of relief. After Thursday, we'll coast on leftovers, "fun" foods, and meals with family and friends until next week—I just need to get over that finish line.

As well as being quick and easy, stir-fries are great because they're so flexible. You can use virtually any veggies, and in any quantities. Stir-fries are also an ideal vehicle for fridge stand-bys cabbage and carrots, which may be all we have left in the crisper by this point (in case you didn't know: they last for weeks).

Since stir-fries are so versatile in this way, I encourage you to approach these recipes as guidelines. Substitute the veggies that you have and like. You'll see that the recipes I've provided here contain a range of techniques, which is how I ensure variety and prevent stir-fry fatigue. These techniques include using cornstarch dissolved in water to thicken stir-fry sauce (like in my Garlic-Soy Tofu with Mushrooms and Napa Cabbage, page 197); coating tofu in cornstarch before frying, then adding sauce to glaze it (Sweet and Sticky Tofu, page 200); using nut butters as the sauce base to change up the protein source (as you'll see in my Saucy Almond-Lime Skillet Veggies, page 206); and stir-frying soaked noodles to create a chewy, flavourful noodle dish (Stir-Fried Peanut Noodles, page 203).

I've also included a couple of the tofu and noodle soups we love: Weeknight Pho-Inspired Noodle Soup (page 207) and Miso Ramen (page 208). These aren't stir-fries, but they hold a similar place in my heart as both a cook and an eater. I generally make them on Thursdays.

How to Cook Tofu

If I had a dollar for every time someone asked me how on earth to cook tofu, I would be a hundredaire at least. I would spend it all on tofu.

There are many schools of thought on how to prepare tofu, and in my decades of eating it regularly, I've tried all of them. Some say to press tofu by layering it in absorbent tea towels and putting heavy things on top, then letting it sit there for a while. I don't generally do this—too time-consuming and ultimately unnecessary. Some say to freeze tofu to alter its texture so it becomes more spongy and absorbs more marinade, and to then marinate it. I don't do this either. Tofu has a wonderful texture, and anyway, one of the many things I love about tofu is its convenience—and freezing, thawing, then marinating something is decidedly inconvenient when you can just cook it straight from the package. Some swear by marinating tofu for hours. I don't find this makes enough of a difference to be worth the extra effort and foresight. Plus, you need a solid amount of marinade to immerse the tofu, which becomes diluted and tofu-ey from the packing water the tofu came in and is therefore, unless you make a special effort to use it, likely to go to waste.

So, what do I do instead?

Start with good tofu

Different brands of tofu will have different tastes and textures. I like it to have a mild, faintly sweet aroma out of the package. Local brands I like are Soyganic and Superior Tofu, but there are many great ones all around the world. If you can access fresh tofu—tofu that hasn't even been sealed in a package—please buy some, or better yet, send some to me. It's absolutely delicious. In general, I stir-fry extra-firm tofu. Medium-firm tofu falls apart if you try to brown it, though it's great cut into chunks and boiled in soups.

Rinse it, then pat dry

Packaged tofu comes sealed with water, which tends to have a pungent, non-delicious taste. Rinse it off. Then pat the tofu dry using a clean tea towel so that it doesn't stick when you cook it, and to start making room for actual flavour.

Cut it strategically

One way to intensify the flavour of tofu is to cut it thinly, which increases the surface area and thus the flavour potential. Cut the tofu into thinnish bite-sized pieces or slabs, especially if you're cooking for someone who is skeptical of tofu.

Consider coating it in (organic) cornstarch

Wet things stick in skillets and don't brown as well. Coating tofu in cornstarch does two things: it helps absorb some of that wetness, so the tofu doesn't stick, and it browns into a lovely crisp exterior. Choose organic cornstarch if avoiding genetically modified organisms (GMOs) is important to you.

Brown it, then add flavour

I find tofu browns best over medium-high heat. Once it has browned a bit, it will be quite dry, and a sponge for flavourful sauces. At this point, I generally like to season the tofu with soy sauce before moving on to prepare the rest of the dish. The soy sauce absorbs quickly. Then, if you want to keep the exterior of the tofu crisp, remove it from the pan and serve it on the side. Otherwise, simply add the rest of your stir-fry ingredients, understanding that if vegetables release liquid or create steam, they'll soften the crisp exterior.

Miso-Chili Oil

Makes ¼ cup (60 mL)

Since I'm feeding kids, I hold back on spicy ingredients when I cook. This spicy, intensely flavourful sauce is a great way to add extra kick for the spice-loving adults. I find that a little goes a long way.

1. Put all the ingredients into a jar or bowl and whisk together, using a fork or small whisk. This oil will store for several weeks in the fridge—give it a good stir before using.

1 Tbsp (15 mL) miso

1 Tbsp (15 mL) soy sauce

1 Tbsp (15 mL) sesame oil

½ Tbsp (7 mL) extra virgin olive oil

½ Tbsp (7 mL) water

1 tsp (5 mL) crushed red chilies, or to taste

Garlic-Soy Tofu with Mushrooms and Napa Cabbage

Serves 4

I make this stir-fry more than any other—it's fast to put together, it's versatile if you want to sub a little of this or that, and it tastes like so much more than the sum of its parts. Everyone in my family is happy when this is dinner. I like using napa cabbage because it's so mild and it virtually disappears into the dish; unsuspecting kids will have no idea how much cabbage they're eating.

1. Heat a wok or large skillet over medium-high heat. Add the oil and then tofu to the pan. Shake the pan to help release the tofu and use a wooden spatula to turn it until it is brown on a few sides.

2. Add 1 Tbsp (15 mL) soy sauce and toss until it is mostly absorbed, 20 to 30 seconds.

3. Add the mushrooms, cabbage, garlic, and several grinds of black pepper. The veggies will release their water and start to soften in 2 to 3 minutes.

4. In a small bowl, whisk the cornstarch with the water, and pour the mixture into the stir-fry along with the remaining 3 Tbsp (45 mL) soy sauce. Cook just until sauce has thickened and all is well combined. If the sauce is too thick, add water 1 Tbsp (15 mL) at a time until it is thinned to your liking.

5. Refrigerate any leftovers in an airtight container for 3 to 4 days.

2 to 3 tsp (10 to 15 mL) avocado oil

1 (12 oz/350 g) block extra-firm tofu, sliced into thin bite-sized pieces and patted dry

4 Tbsp (60 mL) soy sauce, divided

8 oz (225 g) cremini mushrooms or 6 oz (170 g) shiitake mushrooms, destemmed and sliced (about 2½ cups/625 mL)

12 oz (340 g) napa cabbage, thinly sliced (about 5 heaping cups/1.375 L)

8 cloves garlic, minced

Black pepper

1 Tbsp (15 mL) cornstarch

2 Tbsp (30 mL) water

Make it a meal

Serve on top of rice or noodles. If you have them, green onion, toasted sesame seeds, and chili-garlic sauce make nice garnishes.

Healthier Fried Brown Rice

Serves 3 to 4

My kids absolutely love fried rice, and for my part I love that it's a complete meal in a pan that is so quick to make. I often make this for lunches, too. It's important to use rice that has been cooked and then refrigerated, so the grains separate easily and don't clump or become mushy. Whenever I cook rice, I make enough for leftovers so there's some in the fridge later in the week to make fried rice.

1. Heat a large skillet over medium-high heat. Add the oil and tofu. Shake the pan and flip the tofu occasionally, until browned on a few sides. Stir in 1 Tbsp (15 mL) soy sauce to season the tofu.

2. Reduce the heat to medium. Add the peas and corn, and cook until they're nearly tender, 3 to 4 minutes. Add water 1 Tbsp (15 mL) at a time if needed to keep the peas from drying out or sticking to the pan.

3. Stir in the brown rice and cook until heated through, about 2 minutes. Add the remaining 2 Tbsp (30 mL) soy sauce.

4. Turn off the heat and stir in the sesame oil.

5. Refrigerate any leftovers in an airtight container for 3 to 4 days.

2 to 3 tsp (10 to 15 mL) avocado oil

6 oz (175 g) extra-firm tofu, patted dry and cut into ⅓-inch (1 cm) cubes

3 Tbsp (45 mL) soy sauce, divided

¾ cup (185 mL) frozen green peas

½ cup (125 mL) frozen corn kernels

3 cups (750 mL) cooked brown rice (ideally that has been refrigerated)

2 tsp (10 mL) toasted sesame oil

Sweet and Sticky Tofu

Serves 3 to 4 as part of a meal

This dish is a major hit in my house. It's inspired by teriyaki, the ingenious Japanese cooking technique of glazing foods with a sweet and savoury sauce. My simple Canadianized version uses wholesome ingredients that are accessible in my corner of the world. Warning: You may need to double this recipe if you're cooking for kids, otherwise they might eat all of it and you won't get any.

1. In a small bowl, whisk together 1 Tbsp (15 mL) cornstarch with the water until dissolved. Add the soy sauce, maple syrup, and garlic powder and whisk to combine. Set aside the sauce.

2. In a large, wide bowl, evenly dredge the tofu in the remaining 3 Tbsp (45 mL) cornstarch, shaking off any excess.

3. Heat a wide skillet over medium-high heat. Add the oil and dredged tofu.

4. After a minute, shake the pan to see if the tofu releases easily, and if it does, flip it. Continue to shake and flip until most sides are browned.

5. When the tofu is browned, reduce the heat to medium, whisk the sauce again, and pour it into the pan. It will bubble and thicken almost immediately. Continue to cook for 30 seconds to 1 minute to thoroughly cook off the raw cornstarch taste. Serve immediately; this tofu is best when fresh.

4 Tbsp (60 mL) cornstarch, divided (see Tip)

½ cup (125 mL) water

¼ cup (60 mL) soy sauce

3 Tbsp (45 mL) pure maple syrup

1 tsp (5 mL) garlic powder

1 (12 oz/350 g) block extra-firm tofu, sliced into bite-sized pieces and patted dry

3 to 4 tsp (15 to 20 mL) avocado oil

Tip

If you can't tolerate cornstarch, you can substitute potato starch. Do not substitute arrowroot starch, which becomes very sticky when pan-fried (I learned this the hard way).

Variation

With crisp veggies: Add veggies that are good lightly cooked, like snap peas and peppers, to the pan with the tofu in the final minute of browning, before adding the sauce.

Make it a meal

Scoop the tofu and sauce onto a bed of rice and serve with steamed broccoli or bok choy, or a crunchy cabbage slaw made with rice vinegar.

Stir-Fried Peanut Noodles

Serves 3 to 4

When I was a law student, I did a food security internship in rural Thailand and Laos. I often ordered stir-fried noodles from tiny roadside stalls, and I noticed that the vendors never used boiled noodles. Instead, noodles are soaked in unheated water, then cooked along with the stir-fry, where they are a sponge for flavour and take on a deliciously chewy texture. I love to cook rice noodles this way now. These creamy, tangy noodles are a family favourite, and we have them often.

1. In a small bowl, whisk together the peanut butter, soy sauce, and vinegar. Whisk in the water.

2. Heat a large skillet or wok over medium-high heat. Add the oil, cabbage, and carrot and sauté until the cabbage begins to sweat, 1 minute or less.

3. Add the noodles and peanut sauce. Cook, turning often with tongs, until the sauce is absorbed and the noodles are soft (have a bite to test), about 5 minutes. Add splashes of water if needed to prevent the noodles from sticking to the pan and to maintain a smooth sauce consistency.

4. Garnish as you like and serve.

5. Refrigerate any leftovers in an airtight container for 3 to 5 days, reheating in a saucepan or skillet with 1 to 2 Tbsp (15 to 30 mL) water to loosen the noodles and smooth out the sauce.

½ cup (125 mL) natural peanut butter

¼ cup (60 mL) soy sauce

2 Tbsp (30 mL) rice vinegar

1 cup (250 mL) water

2 to 3 tsp (10 to 15 mL) avocado oil

3 cups (750 mL) finely sliced napa cabbage (see Tip)

1 large carrot, grated

½ lb (225 g) medium-width rice noodles, soaked in room-temperature water for 30 minutes

Chili flakes, lime wedges, cilantro, chopped peanuts, flaky finishing salt, to garnish (optional)

Tip

Napa cabbage is incredible: it's nutritious but also quite mild in flavour. When cooked, it virtually disappears into stir-fries. This makes it an ideal leafy green to feed children and vegetable skeptics. However, not every grocer stocks napa cabbage; if you can't find it, use regular green cabbage instead, and expect it to be a firmer cabbage experience.

Five Spice Noodles
with Bok Choy and Tofu

Serves 3 to 4

This easy stir-fry is a good use of plain leftover noodles, which I often have in my fridge from lunches for the boys. You can make them fresh too, of course. Pungent, fragrant five spice—a blend of star anise, cloves, cinnamon, Sichuan pepper, and fennel seeds—is one of my favourite spice blends. If you haven't cooked with it, you'll recognize the aroma and flavour if you've ever eaten at a Chinese or Vietnamese restaurant. It beautifully complements noodles and greens—in this case, bok choy.

1. Heat a large skillet over medium-high heat. Add the oil and tofu and fry the tofu until browned on both sides. Add ½ Tbsp (7 mL) soy sauce and toss to coat. It will absorb quickly.

2. Add the white and light-green parts of the onion, bok choy, and five spice. Cook, stirring often, until the bok choy is wilted and the onion is tender-crisp, about 2 minutes.

3. Reduce the heat to medium-low. Add the noodles, remaining ¼ cup (60 mL) soy sauce, and sesame oil. Use tongs to mix everything together, heating just until the noodles are warmed through, about 1 minute. Immediately remove from the heat so that it does not overcook. Serve, garnishing with the dark-green onion.

4. Refrigerate any leftovers in the fridge for up to 3 days. To reheat, place in a skillet over medium heat with 1 to 2 Tbsp (15 to 30 mL) water.

2 to 3 tsp (10 to 15 mL) avocado oil

6 oz (175 g) extra-firm tofu, sliced into thin bite-sized pieces and patted dry

¼ cup (60 mL) + ½ Tbsp (7 mL) soy sauce, divided

2 green onions, chopped, white and light-green parts separated from dark-green parts

½ lb (225 g) bok choy, chopped and rinsed (about 4 cups/ 1 L loosely packed)

¾ tsp (3 mL) five spice powder

½ lb (225 g) noodles—like rice, soba, ramen, or even linguine— cooked and rinsed in cold water

1 Tbsp (15 mL) sesame oil

Saucy Almond-Lime Skillet Veggies

Serves 4

Tender-crisp veggies smothered in a rich, creamy, and tangy sauce—even vegetable skeptics are won over. I could just about eat the almond-lime sauce with a spoon. The sauce may seem on the thin side at first, but it will thicken in the hot pan, winding up just right. There is enough sauce to generously coat the veggies, with plenty to flavour any grain or starch you pair them with.

1. In a small bowl, whisk together the almond butter, soy sauce, lime juice, and maple syrup. Whisk in the water.

2. Heat a large skillet or wok over medium-high or high heat. Add the oil and veggies and stir-fry until tender-crisp, 5 to 7 minutes.

3. Reduce the heat to medium and pour in the almond-lime sauce, heating just to warm it through. If it seems too thick, add water 1 Tbsp (15 mL) at a time until your desired consistency is reached.

Make it a meal

Serve this stir-fry on top of brown rice, soba or rice noodles, quinoa, or any other grain or starch you like.

½ cup (125 mL) natural almond butter

¼ cup (60 mL) soy sauce

Juice of 1 lime (about 2 Tbsp/ 30 mL)

1 Tbsp (15 mL) pure maple syrup

½ cup (125 mL) water

2 to 3 tsp (10 to 15 mL) avocado oil

8 cups (2 L) stir-fry veggies, sliced or cubed into bite-sized pieces—I like snap peas, green beans, green or napa cabbage, bell peppers, carrot (thinly sliced), broccoli, mushrooms, and white or red onions

Weeknight Pho-Inspired Noodle Soup

Serves 3 to 4

As a lifelong soup lover, naturally I swooned the first time I tasted brothy, fragrant pho with slurpy noodles and ample tender-crisp vegetables. For years as a young student I was a regular at my local Vietnamese restaurant, where a bowl of perfectly balanced vegetarian pho never failed to soothe my soul. Five spice—of which I sang the praises on page 204—makes an easy weeknight stand-in to capture pho's essence. The hoisin adds saltiness and complexity, so if you don't have it and plan to skip it, you may want to add an extra drizzle of soy sauce in its place.

1. Boil a large pot of water and cook the noodles according to the package directions. Drain, rinse, and set aside.

2. Meanwhile, heat a large pot over medium to medium-low heat. Add the oil and ginger and sauté until the ginger has turned a few shades darker, 1 to 2 minutes. The oil should be bubbling around the ginger.

3. Add the onion and mushrooms and increase the heat to medium-high. They will stick to the bottom of the pot and brown deeply. Cook for 3 to 4 minutes, until soft and very fragrant.

4. Add the water, deglazing the pan by scraping up any stuck browned bits from the bottom of the pan with a wooden spoon. Add the five spice and soy sauce. Bring mixture to a boil, then reduce the heat to medium-low to simmer, covered, for 10 minutes.

5. Add the assorted veggies and simmer for another 2 minutes, or until the veggies are just crisp-tender.

6. Divide the noodles among four bowls. Ladle the broth and veggies over the noodles. Add a handful of bean sprouts and a few basil leaves to each bowl. Serve with lime wedges, hoisin sauce, and chili-garlic sauce at the table.

7. Refrigerate noodle and broth leftovers separately in airtight containers for 2 to 3 days.

½ lb (225 g) thin rice noodles

2 to 3 tsp (10 to 15 mL) avocado oil

1 scant Tbsp (13 mL) minced ginger

½ medium white onion, slivered

1 heaping cup (275 mL) shiitake mushrooms, sliced and destemmed (about 2½ oz/75 g)

8 cups (2 L) water

1 tsp (5 mL) five spice powder

2 Tbsp (30 mL) soy sauce

3 cups (750 mL) assorted cut veggies, such as broccoli florets, thinly sliced carrot, slivered red bell pepper

Mung bean sprouts, basil (Thai basil if available), lime wedges, hoisin sauce, and chili-garlic sauce, to garnish

Miso Ramen

Serves 4

Ramen—Japanese noodle soup—is so delicious that, across the globe, entire restaurants are devoted to serving only different versions of it. I love to make it with miso, which creates a naturally hearty, savoury, and tangy broth. From the minute the aromatics start sautéing in sesame oil and filling the house with their intoxicating scent, my family starts to ask, "how long until dinner?!" Fortunately, they don't need to wait long, because this simple soup comes together very quickly.

1. Boil a large pot of water and cook the noodles according to the package directions. Drain and set aside.

2. Meanwhile, heat a large pot over medium-low heat. Add the sesame oil, garlic, ginger, and the white and light-green parts of the onion. Allow the garlic and ginger to slowly brown for a couple of minutes—they should sizzle but not smoke. The onion will soften.

3. Stir in the mushrooms along with the salt. The mushrooms should start to sweat in a couple of minutes.

4. Add the soy sauce and allow it to soak into the mushrooms for a few seconds, then add the water and tofu. Bring to a boil, reduce the heat to medium-low, and simmer for 5 minutes, partially covered, to incorporate the flavours.

5. Turn off the heat. Ladle about 1 cup (250 mL) of the broth into a bowl. Add the miso and whisk to dissolve it. Pour the mixture into the pot and stir to combine.

6. Divide the cooked noodles among four bowls. Ladle the soup over the noodles and garnish with the dark-green onion.

7. Refrigerate noodle and broth leftovers separately in airtight containers for 2 to 3 days.

4 servings ramen noodles, about 10 oz (300 g) dried

2 Tbsp (30 mL) sesame oil

3 cloves garlic, minced

1½ Tbsp (22 mL) minced ginger

2 green onions, chopped, white and light-green parts separated from dark-green parts

4 oz (110 g) shiitake mushrooms, destemmed and thinly sliced (2 heaping cups/550 mL)

Pinch of salt

2 Tbsp (30 mL) soy sauce

8 cups (2 L) water

1 (12 oz/350 g) block medium-firm tofu, cut into ¾-inch (2 cm) cubes

6 Tbsp (90 mL) miso (see Tips)

Tips

I like Hikari Miso brand white (aka "white type") miso.

Since 4 Tbsp (60 mL) is equivalent to ¼ cup, I find that the easiest way to measure out the 6 Tbsp (90 mL) miso is to fill a ¼-cup (60 mL) measure one and a half times. Measurements math!

Snacks and Sweets

To live in a house with kids is to require a steady stream of snacks and sweets. In our daily lives, probably as with many people, our snacks are often simple foods: fruit, raw veggies, crackers, nuts. I typically make Oil-Free Hummus (page 214) or White Bean Purée (page 215) at least once a week, because they're nutritious, portable, filling, and inexpensive. And both of my kids absolutely love Crispy Chickpea Flatbread (page 216), which is also a fun snack to put out for company.

Although there is absolutely a role for sugar-sweetened treats like cake and ice cream, most of the time, I like to satisfy sweet cravings with nutritious foods that go undercover as treats. A Better Chocolate Chip Cookie (page 223) contains wholesome ingredients but feels so decadent. Even the Cinnamon Baked Bananas on page 227 are so sweet and delicious, it somehow feels like cheating.

In my mind, the ultimate sweet is one that could qualify as a breakfast food as much as a dessert. In fact, sometimes we do have Peanut Butter Caramel Corn (page 218) or Whole Foods Any-Fruit Crumble (page 228) for breakfast! And Banana Chip Muffins (page 220) make sense at pretty much any time of day—they're especially perfect for school lunches.

Oil-Free Hummus

Makes 1¾ cups (435 mL)

If I could only bring one food to a desert island, it would probably be hummus. It's delicious, versatile, portable, kid-friendly, and incredibly nutritious, with plant-based protein, iron made more absorptive from the vitamin C in the lemons, and a slew of other vitamins and minerals. We eat a lot of hummus in our house, since it's such a perfect snack, so I often make double or triple batches.

I highly recommend cooking chickpeas from dried for this. You can cook them until they're very soft and then blend them while still warm, both of which help create a creamy hummus. Plus, using the liquid the chickpeas cooks in contributes body and flavour. In a pinch, canned will be fine. Ideally, look for cans without added preservatives, or consider draining and rinsing the chickpeas, then using water instead of chickpea cooking liquid to eliminate that canned flavour.

I know this may be controversial, but I don't generally add garlic to hummus. I find it can be overpowering, especially after being in the fridge for a day. But, of course, feel free to add a clove or two, if you'd like.

1. Add the chickpeas and cooking liquid or water to a blender or food processor and blend for at least 2 or 3 minutes. Even when the chickpeas seem puréed, keep going!

2. Add the tahini, lemon juice, and salt and continue to blend, adding more chickpea cooking liquid or water 1 Tbsp (15 mL) at a time until your desired consistency is reached. Taste and adjust the flavours.

3. Refrigerate any leftovers in an airtight container for up to 4 days.

1½ cups (375 mL) cooked chickpeas

3 Tbsp (45 mL) chickpea cooking liquid or water, plus more as needed (see Tip)

¼ cup (60 mL) tahini

1½ Tbsp (22 mL) freshly squeezed lemon juice (about ½ lemon), plus more to taste

½ tsp (2 mL) salt

Tip

I prefer hummus to be on the thicker side when using it as a dip, but if I'm planning to use it for bowls, I'll make it nearly pourable. Either way is wonderful. If you find it too thick after being in the fridge, simply whisk in water a splash at a time until you like the consistency.

White Bean Purée

Makes 1½ cups (375 mL)

Although hummus has a well-deserved, iconic spot in our collective bean purée culinary repertoire, really, you can purée just about any bean with a bit of salt, oil, and acid to make a delicious dip. I love this white bean purée for dipping crackers and raw veggies in, and for dolloping onto bowls as my legume. Neutral cannellini beans allow the lemon, olive oil, and garlic to pop while creating an unbeatably creamy base. Double the recipe if you're as serious about bean purées as I am.

1. Put all the ingredients in a blender or food processor and process until smooth.
2. Refrigerate in an airtight container for up to 4 days. The purée will thicken in the fridge.

1½ cups (375 mL) cooked cannellini (white kidney) beans

¼ cup (60 mL) bean cooking liquid or water

1 Tbsp (15 mL) extra virgin olive oil

1½ Tbsp (22 mL) freshly squeezed lemon juice (about ½ lemon)

¼ tsp (1 mL) salt

1 clove garlic, plus more to taste

Variation

Herby White Bean Purée: Add a handful of parsley, basil, or cilantro for a flavourful green version.

Crispy Chickpea Flatbread

Serves 4 as a snack

Socca is a popular snack in southern France, served by street vendors and eaten with your hands, and it's the inspiration for this recipe. This is a go-to dish for lazy afternoons when we have friends or family over, or as part of a casual, snacky meal. It's also very pantry-friendly; it has saved me many times when the fridge was looking a little sparse and I wanted to make something filling and protein-rich for my kids. The flavour and texture are improved by allowing the batter to sit for at least 10 minutes or even up to several hours, so don't be afraid to make the batter ahead of time. Enjoy fresh out of the oven, when the edges are crisp and the interior, flaky.

1. Preheat the oven to 450°F (230°C).

2. In a medium bowl, whisk together the chickpea flour, salt, and water. Set the mixture aside to allow the flour to hydrate while the oven preheats.

3. Add the oil to a 12-inch (30 cm) cast iron skillet (see Tip) and swirl around to fully coat the bottom and a ½ inch (1.2 cm) up the sides. Gently pour the batter into the pan.

4. Bake for 12 to 14 minutes, or until the flatbread is matte and starting to brown on top, then broil for 2 to 3 more minutes, until the top is golden.

5. Using a spatula, slide onto a cutting board and slice into pieces. Enjoy while fresh.

1 cup (250 mL) chickpea flour
½ tsp (2 mL) salt
1¼ cups (310 mL) water
2 Tbsp (30 mL) avocado oil

Tip

If you don't have a 12-inch (30 cm) cast iron skillet, a 9- × 13-inch (3.5 L) baking dish works too—just be aware that the flatbread won't be as crispy, and you may not be able to slide it onto a cutting board. If that's the case, serve it directly from the baking dish.

Peanut Butter Caramel Corn

Serves 4

The combination of peanut butter and maple syrup tastes uncannily like caramel. Better maybe, since it has a little more dimension and less cloying sweetness than traditional caramel. We make a lot of popcorn in our house because it's low waste, easy, and delicious. It's also nutritious: popcorn is a whole grain, and a good source of iron and zinc, among other minerals and vitamins. We often dress popcorn simply with extra virgin olive oil, nutritional yeast, and salt. But when we're in the mood for something more decadent, this peanut butter caramel corn is a beloved go-to. Arden will even sometimes make it for the boys for breakfast.

1. Preheat the oven to 300°F (150°C).

2. Pop the popcorn kernels (see Tip) and transfer to a very large bowl, leaving behind any unpopped kernels so they don't make it into the caramel corn.

3. In a small bowl, whisk together the peanut butter, maple syrup, oil, vanilla, and salt. Pour over the popcorn and mix. I find this easiest to do with my (clean) hands.

4. Spread the coated popcorn on a baking sheet and bake for 14 minutes, or until the sauce has dried and turned a few shades darker. Allow to cool for 5 to 10 minutes, until crisp.

5. Store in an airtight container and enjoy within a day.

½ cup (125 mL) popcorn kernels

⅓ cup (80 mL) peanut butter

⅓ cup (80 mL) pure maple syrup

1 Tbsp (15 mL) extra virgin olive oil

2 tsp (10 mL) pure vanilla extract

¼ tsp (1 mL) salt

Tip

We use an air popper, which is one of our most-used appliances. I popped corn on a stovetop for many years, though, and it's a good option, too. To pop corn on the stove, heat a thin layer of oil and test 2 kernels over medium heat in a saucepan with the lid sliiiiightly ajar to let steam escape. When the test kernels pop, add enough kernels to just cover the bottom of the pan, return the lid to its slightly ajar position, and shake to coat the kernels with the oil. Allow the popcorn to pop—popping should slow to several seconds apart—before removing from heat.

Banana Chip Muffins

Makes 12 muffins

Nut-free and perfect for tucking into school lunches and summer picnic baskets, these muffins are lightly sweet and super moist. My kids devour them! On my end, I feel good about the relatively wholesome ingredients and how quickly they come together, thanks to the blender.

1. Preheat the oven to 350°F (175°C) and brush a 12-cup muffin tin with oil or line with paper liners.

2. Put the oats, milk, bananas, maple syrup, tahini, and vanilla in a blender, and blend on low until smooth.

3. In a large bowl, whisk together the flour, baking powder, cinnamon, and salt. Pour the wet ingredients into the dry and stir to combine. Fold in the chocolate chips.

4. Distribute the batter evenly among the prepared muffin cups.

5. Bake for 25 minutes, or until the tops of the muffins are browned and spring back when gently pressed.

6. Store in airtight container for 1 to 2 days at room temperature, 5 to 7 days in the fridge, or up to 3 months in the freezer.

1 cup (250 mL) rolled oats

1 cup (250 mL) plant-based milk

2 ripe bananas

⅓ cup (80 mL) pure maple syrup

⅓ cup (80 mL) tahini

1 tsp (5 mL) pure vanilla extract

1 cup (250 mL) gluten-free all-purpose baking flour (see Tip)

2 tsp (10 mL) baking powder

1 tsp (5 mL) cinnamon

½ tsp (2 mL) salt

½ cup (125 mL) dairy-free dark chocolate chips

Tip

We use Bob's Red Mill Gluten-Free All-Purpose Baking Flour. This flour bakes up like refined-wheat all-purpose flour, but the first ingredient is chickpea flour! Win.

A Better Chocolate Chip Cookie

Makes 14 to 16 cookies

My husband, Arden, has a major sweet tooth. Since we started carefully reading food labels and thinking more about what we put into our bodies, we've been on a constant quest to find foods that satisfy sweet cravings using more wholesome ingredients. Sweet-toothed Arden has been making some version of these tender, decadent cookies regularly for 10 years. Our kids can't get enough of them, either.

1. Preheat the oven to 350°F (175°C) and oil a baking sheet or line it with parchment paper.

2. In a large bowl, whisk together the oat flour, baking soda, and salt.

3. Make a well in the centre of the dry ingredients. Add the tahini, maple syrup, and vanilla. Combine the wet ingredients a little before incorporating them into the dry ingredients and mixing thoroughly. Fold in the chocolate chips. Don't worry about overworking the dough; it doesn't contain gluten and so can't become tough.

4. Scoop heaping tablespoons (20 mL) of dough onto the prepared baking sheet, gently flattening into disks with your clean hand. (Wet your hand with water to make this easier.)

5. Bake for 8 to 10 minutes, or until a quick peek using a spatula reveals that the bottom has browned. Allow the cookies to rest on the baking sheet out of the oven for 5 to 10 minutes before transferring to a wire rack to cool completely.

6. Store in an airtight container at room temperature for up to 3 days or in the freezer for up to 3 months.

1¼ cups (310 mL) oat flour (see Tip)

½ tsp (2 mL) baking soda

¼ tsp (1 mL) salt

½ cup (125 mL) tahini

½ cup (125 mL) pure maple syrup

1 Tbsp (15 mL) pure vanilla extract

¼ cup (60 mL) dairy-free dark chocolate chips

Tip

To make oat flour, simply put rolled oats in a blender and blend on high until finely ground.

Variation

Peanut Butter Chip Cookies: These are delicious with peanut butter in place of tahini.

Simple Chocolate Almond Cookies

Makes 10 small cookies

Almond flour is great for baking because it naturally contains fat, so not only does it act as a flour, it also provides richness and some moisture. Almond flour is also incredibly nutritious: it contains vitamin E, magnesium, iron, and calcium, and is rich in protein. These chocolatey, lightly sweet cookies are both delicious and satiating. I love one or two of them after lunch with my afternoon tea.

1. Preheat the oven to 350°F (175°C) and oil a baking sheet or line it with parchment paper.

2. In a large bowl, stir together the almond flour, cocoa powder, and salt, using the back of your spoon to mash up any clumps of flour.

3. Add the maple syrup, vanilla, and water, stirring well to combine. The dough will seem dry at first, but soon it should just come together. If it doesn't, add water ¼ tsp (1 mL) at a time until it does.

4. Roughly divide the dough into 10 portions. Roll each portion into a ball and then flatten into a disk on the prepared baking sheet with your clean hand. (Wet your hand with water to make this easier.)

5. Bake for 10 to 12 minutes, or until a quick peek using a spatula reveals that the bottom has browned. Allow the cookies to rest on the baking sheet out of the oven for 5 to 10 minutes before moving to a wire rack to cool completely. Store in an airtight container at room temperature for up to 3 days or in the freezer for up to 3 months.

1½ cups (375 mL) almond flour

2 Tbsp (30 mL) cocoa powder

Pinch of salt

3 Tbsp (45 mL) pure maple syrup

2 tsp (10 mL) pure vanilla extract

1 Tbsp (15 mL) water

One-Ingredient Watermelon Popsicles

Makes 6 popsicles

Watermelons are one of our favourite summer fruits, sweet and juicy and so refreshing on a hot day. We take slices to the beach and let the juice run where it will, then jump into the water to rinse off. I also love that watermelons are full of vitamins (including vitamins A and C) and phytonutrients (including lycopene). Inevitably, toward the end of the summer, watermelons start to get a bit mealy. This is the perfect time to make watermelon popsicles!

1. Place the watermelon in a blender and blend until very smooth. Pour into popsicle moulds and freeze until solid, 2 to 4 hours. Drink any juice remaining in the blender—it's absolutely delicious!

3 cups (750 mL) seedless watermelon chunks, cut in 1-inch (2.5 cm) cubes

Variations

With berries: Add a handful of strawberries or raspberries to change up the flavour.

With lime: For a more grown-up flavour, add 1 tsp (5 mL) lime zest and the juice of ½ lime (1 Tbsp/15 mL).

Cinnamon Baked Bananas

Serves 2

Gooey soft bananas, caramelized maple syrup, and a cozy cinnamon aroma. This is one of those easy dishes that tastes better than you'd expect given how simple it is—my kind of cooking. It's elegant enough for a special occasion, although you might want to add a scoop of vegan ice cream for good measure. The recipe scales up easily.

1. Preheat the oven to 400°F (200°C).

2. Peel the bananas and cut in half lengthwise. Arrange in a small baking dish cut side up. Drizzle evenly with the maple syrup and vanilla, and sprinkle with the cinnamon.

3. Bake for 15 minutes, or until the sauce is bubbling and the bananas are very soft.

2 ripe bananas
2 tsp (10 mL) pure maple syrup
¾ tsp (3 mL) pure vanilla extract
½ tsp (2 mL) cinnamon

Variations

This is a versatile recipe, perfect for adapting and playing around with.

- Add 1 Tbsp (15 mL) rum or whisky.
- Skip the maple syrup, or replace it with coconut or cane sugar.
- Sprinkle on ½ tsp (2 mL) cocoa powder along with or instead of the cinnamon.
- Use 1 Tbsp (15 mL) citrus juice—lime, lemon, or orange—instead of the vanilla.

Whole Foods Any-Fruit Crumble

Serves 4 to 6

My love of foraging and growing is no secret among those who know me, and I'm often lucky to be invited to pick from fruit trees or bushes that friends can't keep up with. I've also grown up picking from the wild blackberry brambles that grow all around southwestern British Columbia. Whenever I come into an abundance of fruit, I make crumbles, just like my mum did. I love to eat leftovers of this delicious whole foods crumble for breakfast, cold from the fridge on hot summer days.

1. Preheat the oven to 350°F (175°C).

2. Combine the fruit, 2 tsp (10 mL) arrowroot powder or cornstarch, and 2 Tbsp (30 mL) maple syrup in an 8- × 8-inch (2 L) baking dish. If the fruit you're using is especially juicy, add an extra 1 tsp (5 mL) arrowroot powder or cornstarch.

3. In a medium bowl, add the oats, almond flour, remaining 2 Tbsp (30 mL) maple syrup, and tahini. Use a fork to toss the ingredients together, mashing to break up any clumps, until the mixture is well combined.

4. Spoon the crumble topping evenly over the fruit filling. Bake for 35 minutes, or until the filling is bubbling and the topping is browned. Transfer to a wire rack to let cool and firm up for 10 to 15 minutes before serving.

5 cups (1.25 L) fruit of your choice, pitted and chopped into bite-sized pieces if necessary (see Tip)

2 to 3 tsp (10 to 15 mL) arrowroot powder or cornstarch

4 Tbsp (60 mL) maple syrup, divided

¾ cup (185 mL) rolled oats

½ cup (125 mL) almond flour

1 Tbsp (15 mL) tahini

Tip

What fruit to use? One of the beautiful things about crumble is that it's so flexible and can be a catch-all for whatever fruit you happen to have an abundance of. I sometimes use frozen fruit to round out whatever fresh fruit I have, or to add refined-sugar-free sweetness. Great crumble fruits include apples, pears, plums, peaches, nectarines, blackberries, cherries, strawberries, blueberries, and rhubarb. Combine firmer fruits (like apples) with soft berries. Combine sweeter fruits with tart ones. Some of my go-to combinations are blackberry apple, strawberry rhubarb, and frozen mixed berries with frozen cherries when fresh fruit isn't available.

End Notes

1. Sarah Gray, "Cooking with Extra Virgin Olive Oil," *ACNEM Journal* 34, 2 (2015): 8–12; Leslie Beck, "What Is Smoke Point and Does It Matter When Cooking with Oil?" *Globe and Mail*, September 28, 2015*l*.

2. Apicius, *Cookery and Dining in Imperial Rome*, trans. Joseph Dommers Vehling (e Good Press, 2019).

3. Health Canada, "Sodium in Canada," March 1, 2017 , https://www.canada.ca/en /health-canada/services/food-nutrition/healthy-eating/sodium.html.

4. Teodardo Calles, Maria Xipsiti, and Riccardo del Castello, "Legacy of the International Year of the Pulses," *Environ Earth Sci* 78 (2019), art. no. 124.

5. Ana Sandoiu, "'Largest' Microbiome Study Weighs in on Our Gut Health," *Medical News Today*, May 15, 2018, citing D. McDonald, E. Hyde, Justine W. Debelius, et al., "American Gut: An Open Platform for Citizen Science Microbiome Research," mSystems 3: e00031-18 (May 2018).

6. A.F. Abdull Razis and N.M. Noor, "Cruciferous Vegetables: Dietary Phytochemicals for Cancer Prevention," *Asian Pac J Cancer Prev* 14, 3 (2013): 1565–70.

7. Shivapriya Manchali, Kotamballi N. Chidambara Murthy, and Bhimanagouda S. Patil, "Crucial Facts about Health Benefits of Popular Cruciferous Vegetables," *Journal of Functional Foods* 4, 1 (2012): 94–106.

8. A.S. Axelsson, E. Tubbs, B. Mecham, et al., "Sulforaphane Reduces Hepatic Glucose Production and Improves Glucose Control in Patients with Type 2 Diabetes," *Sci Transl Med* 9, 394 (2017): eaah4477.

9. Y. Sun, T. Yang, L. Mao, and F. Zhang, "Sulforaphane Protects against Brain Diseases: Roles of Cytoprotective Enzymes," *Austin J Cerebrovasc Dis Stroke* 4, 1 (2017): 1054.

10. K. Kleszczyński, I.M. Ernst, A.E. Wagner, et al., "Sulforaphane and Phenylethyl Isothiocyanate Protect Human Skin against UVR-Induced Oxidative Stress and Apoptosis: Role of Nrf2-Dependent Gene Expression and Antioxidant Enzymes," *Pharmacol Res* 78 (2013): 28–40.

11. K. Singh, S.L. Connors, E.A. Macklin, et al., "Sulforaphane Treatment of Autism Spectrum Disorder (ASD)," *Proc Natl Acad Sci USA* 111, 43 (2014): 15550–55.

Acknowledgements

Mark Twain said there is no such thing as a new idea, and that is certainly true with this book. I am indebted to countless food bloggers and columnists, cookbook authors, chefs, YouTubers, and Instagrammers for inspiring me with ingredients and techniques, and for continually re-energizing my passion for delicious, nourishing food from the earth.

I'm especially grateful to the uncelebrated home cooks from food cultures around the world who pioneered preparing vegetables, tubers, grains, lentils, and beans to transform them from edible to delectable. These creative cooks, many of them women and mothers—from Asia to Africa to Central and South America—are the real MVPs. Your legacy brings joy to my kitchen every day.

Thank you to everyone who has supported *Easy Animal-Free* by following and sharing my work, for sending me heartfelt messages or simply being silently present. I knew I had something to say about practical vegan cooking for busy families, but I couldn't have foreseen just how gratifying it would be to become a small part of your kitchens. Food is a common human language, and it unites us even when we aren't eating at the same table.

Zach Berman, you are the master of bringing people together. Thank you for asking me if I'd ever thought about turning *Easy Animal-Free* into a book and if I'd like to be introduced to your publisher. And when I said I didn't see that fitting into my life, thank you for gently nudging me again later. You were absolutely right.

To the incredible team at Appetite by Random House—Robert McCullough, Lindsay Paterson, Rachel Brown, Leah Springate, Judith Phillips, and others—your unseen efforts are what make books beautiful, clear, and consistent. Thank you for believing so wholeheartedly in this book from day one, and for using your considerable talents to help make it a reality.

Erin Ireland, what haven't you done to help me with this book? Thank you for checking in on me and cheering me on every step of the way, for lending me gear and ingredients, for feeding me and letting me feed you, for sharing my work with your own audience, and for always being up for a lengthy conversation about vegan food—our favourite topic. Everyone should be so lucky to have a friend like you.

To my parents, John Pippus and Pam Searle, you raised me to be true to myself and write my own life story, no matter how unorthodox. Thank you for teaching me the value of a home cooked meal shared with loved ones, for embracing plant-based eating with me, and for energetically and enthusiastically entertaining my kids while I wrote and cooked for this book.

Harlan and Alister, my sweet muses, I'm so lucky that I get to be your mama. Thank you for trying (almost) everything I cook, and thank you for being the most delightful, joyful, hilarious dinner companions imaginable. I love feeding you.

To my one and only Arden Beddoes, I've always struggled to find the words to express the depth of my love and gratitude for you. This book, and everything else in my life, rests on the foundation of our partnership. Thank you for your unwavering support, patience, generosity, and humour. And thank you for doing all those dishes.

Index